INTERNATIONAL COPYRIGHT, U.S. & FOREIGN COMMERCIAL SERVICE AND U.S. DEPARTMENT OF STATE, 2010. ALL RIGHTS RESERVED OUTSIDE OF THE UNITED STATES.

- Chapter 1: Doing Business In Singapore
- Chapter 2: Political and Economic Environment
- Chapter 3: Selling U.S. Products and Services
- Chapter 4: Leading Sectors for U.S. Export and Investment
- Chapter 5: Trade Regulations, Customs and Standards
- Chapter 6: Investment Climate
- Chapter 7: Trade and Project Financing
- Chapter 8: Business Travel
- Chapter 9: Contacts, Market Research and Trade Events
- Chapter 10: Guide to Our Services

Return to table of contents

Chapter 1: Doing Business In Singapore

- Market Overview
- Market Challenges
- Market Opportunities
- Market Entry Strategy

Market Overview   Return to top

- Singapore was the United States' 13th largest export market and 17th largest trading partner in 2013. The U.S. goods trade surplus with Singapore jumped 24.7% to nearly $12.9 billion, the highest level ever recorded with Singapore. Exports to Singapore reached $30.7 billion and imports from Singapore were $17.8 billion. The Singapore economy grew by 4.1% in 2013 and the Singapore Government forecasted GDP will expand by 2.0% to 4.0% in 2014.

- During the first 10 years of the U.S. Singapore Free Trade Agreement, which came into effect on January 1, 2004, two-way trade has increased 53% and U.S. exports by nearly 85.4%. The United States is Singapore's 3rd largest supplier of imported goods in 2013. China overtook Malaysia as Singapore's top source of imports and the other major suppliers were Taiwan, South Korea, Japan, Indonesia, United Emirates, Saudi Arabia and Germany.

- Singapore is a participant in the Trans-Pacific Partnership (TPP) negotiations, through which the United States and 11 other Asia-Pacific partners are seeking to establish a comprehensive, next-generation regional agreement to liberalize trade and investment.

Market Challenges   Return to top

- Singapore's open economy attracts suppliers from throughout the world providing tough competition and reducing margins for U.S. suppliers. The country is also seeing increased business costs and a tightening labor market. In response to the concerns voiced by the indigenous population, the government has made a decision to tighten the inflow of foreign workers and has accepted the policy will result in slower growth for the country.

- Despite its liberal trading regime, foreign companies face barriers in certain service sectors such as pay TV, audiovisual and media services, legal services, banking, licensing of online news websites, cloud computing for financial institutions, and healthcare: procedural transparency and fairness. Details can be found in the USTR Report on Foreign Trade Barriers that is available at http://www.ustr.gov/sites/default/files/2014%20NTE%20Report%20on%20FTB%20Singapore.pdf.

Market Opportunities Return to top

- Singapore is one of the best markets in Asia for U.S. companies hoping to expand their market penetration throughout Asia. With a U.S. style of business, strong intellectual property protection, a small, easy to navigate market, an English-speaking society, and virtually no corruption, Singapore is a great regional trading hub.

- U.S. companies will find attractive market opportunities in Singapore for the following best prospects sectors: aircraft and parts, medical devices, computer hardware and software, laboratory and scientific instruments, environment control equipment, oil & gas, telecommunication equipment, education.

- Following are major infrastructure projects, significant government procurements and business opportunities:

    - $500 million second LNG terminal is being planned.

    - $150 million construction of very large floating structures to store oil and petroleum products; decision is expected by end 2014.

    - $280 million blueprint to grow the clean energy industry in Singapore.

    - Construction of a new 300-bed hospital for infectious disease slated for completion by 2018 and a new $135 million National Heart Center Building;

    - Construction of up to 25 public nursing homes by 2020, and four public acute medical care hospitals and up to 12 polyclinics by 2030;

    - Private medical groups will spend more than $406 million to build, expand and upgrade their healthcare facilities;

    - Construction of Singapore Changi Airport Terminal 4 and Terminal 5;

    - $944 million of Singapore government information technology tenders in the Financial Year 2014 (April 2014-March 2015).

Market Entry Strategy Return to top

- Using agents or distributors is a common and effective way to serve the Singapore market and, from here, other countries in Southeast Asia. Many distributors in Singapore deal not only with the local market but also with the broader regional market. Establishing a distributor in Singapore is an excellent way to start looking at the wider Asian market. It is important for U.S. firms to visit their representatives, maintain a good relationship with them and respond quickly to inquiries. Prospective exporters to Singapore should be aware that competition is high and that buyers expect good after-sales service. When business warrants, many companies have found it useful and sometimes necessary to set up offices in Singapore. Singapore is home to over 3,000 American firms, most of which serve the regional market.

Return to table of contents

Return to table of contents

Chapter 2: Political and Economic Environment

For background information on the political and economic environment of the country, please click on the link below to the U.S. Department of State Background Notes.

http://www.state.gov/r/pa/ei/bgn/2798.htm

Return to table of contents

Return to table of contents

Chapter 3: Selling U.S. Products and Services

- Using an Agent or Distributor
- Establishing an Office
- Franchising
- Direct Marketing
- Joint Ventures/Licensing
- Selling to the Government
- Distribution and Sales Channels
- Selling Factors/Techniques
- Electronic Commerce
- Trade Promotion and Advertising
- Pricing
- Sales Service/Customer Support
- Protecting Your Intellectual Property
- Due Diligence
- Local Professional Services
- Web Resources

Using an Agent or Distributor   Return to top

Many American exporters use agents or distributors to serve the Singapore market and other markets in Southeast Asia. Finding prospective partners usually presents no problem as Singapore firms are aggressive when it comes to representing new products and typically respond enthusiastically to new opportunities. Most American companies that use the U.S. Commercial Service (CS) Singapore matchmaking and promotion services in Singapore find several interested agents or distributors. Because of the relatively small size of the Singapore market, potential partners often ask to cover regional territories. With a strong history of trade, Singaporean companies are particularly successful in taking products to the region. CS Singapore offers a wide range of programs and has an excellent record of success in introducing U.S. firms to the market. A list of services offered by CS Singapore can be obtained from our website at www.export.gov/singapore.

Establishing an Office   Return to top

American firms wishing to establish a presence in Singapore have several straightforward options to do so. They can establish a Representative Office (RO), register as a Branch of the parent, or incorporate as a Singapore company. General information on establishing an office can be found at
http://www.enterpriseone.gov.sg/en/Business%20Stages/Start.aspx.

If an American company wishes to carry on operations in Singapore, it should register a branch office or incorporate a local company with the Accounting & Corporate

Regulatory Authority (ACRA) – http://www.acra.gov.sg. ACRA publishes an excellent guide that takes the first time registrant through the process of establishing a branch office or incorporating in Singapore.

Representative Office

Setting up a Representative Office in Singapore can be a good way for American firms to explore business opportunities in Singapore or the region. ROs in banking and insurance need to register with the Monetary Authority of Singapore (MAS) and meet the guidelines or requirements lay out by the MAS. ROs in all other industries need to register with International Enterprise (IE) Singapore.

ROs can only carry out market research, conduct feasibility studies or work as a liaison on behalf of the parent company. RO may not conduct business directly or on behalf of the parent company. ROs cannot ship, transship or store goods in Singapore. American firms can either work through an agent or distributor to do so or establish their own commercial presence.

Branch Office

For Branch Offices, the Companies Act requires a foreign company to appoint two local agents in Singapore to act on behalf of the company. The agents must be ordinarily resident in Singapore i.e. a Singaporean Citizen, a Singapore Permanent Resident, or a person who has been issued an EntrePass/Approval-In-Principle letter/Dependent Pass.

Establishing a Singapore Business

American firms can also register a sole-proprietorship, partnership, limited liability partnership or incorporate a company in Singapore. For a sole proprietorship the process takes about one day, while more complex business entities can take up to six weeks and require lawyers and accountants to assist with incorporation documents. A point to bear in mind is that registration/incorporation of a company does not automatically mean that expatriate staff can be assigned to Singapore. Foreign staff must obtain employment passes from the Singapore Ministry of Manpower, although this is generally quite routine.

Franchising   Return to top

Singapore is home to a wide variety of franchise concepts with more than 500 concepts and over 30,000 franchisees operating in the country. Foreign franchises are well received and the United States is by far the largest supplier of foreign franchises in the country. There are American franchises in practically every industry. McDonald's, Burger King, KFC, Subway, Starbucks, Ben and Jerry's, Gymboree, New Horizons, Mister Minit, Avis, Toys R Us, On-line Trading Academy, Comfort Keepers, Contours Express, and many others have operations in Singapore. American franchises that opened recently in Singapore include Krispy Kreme and Wing Zone.

Singaporeans continue to seek out new franchise concepts to introduce into the country. The success of selling a franchise in Singapore is based on a number of factors including brand name, up-front costs and royalties, the concept's uniqueness and the flexibility of the franchise agreement. U.S. franchisors should note that real estate in Singapore is prohibitively expensive and getting good locations is a challenge, especially for those in the retail and F&B business.

With its strategic location and well-developed infrastructure, Singapore serves as the regional showcase and distribution center for U.S. franchisors wishing to enter the markets of Asia. There have been instances where visitors from the region saw a franchise concept in Singapore and were interested to bring it back to their own countries. In 2013, Singapore attracted over 15 million visitors from around the world. The country's multi-ethnic society also makes the country an ideal location for foreign franchisors to test their concepts and use the reaction to gauge the acceptance of their franchise in Asia. There are also opportunities for U.S. franchisors to work with Singapore companies to access markets in nearby countries. Singapore investors may buy franchise licenses for additional markets in the Southeast Asian region and not for Singapore alone.

Direct Marketing   Return to top

The direct marketing industry in Singapore began in the early 1990s and now includes direct mail, telemarketing, television sales, mail order, call centers, fulfillment and e-commerce firms. The Direct Marketing Association of Singapore represents both users and service providers. The direct marketing industry is well supported by service companies including: Singapore Post, Singapore Telecom Call Center, Teledirect, TNT International Mail, Ogilvy One and MMS Consultancy, among many others. The Singapore government also actively supports the industry by assisting companies (through financial incentives) in using direct marketing for their trading activities through its Direct Marketing Program.

The Direct Selling Association of Singapore (DSAS), a self-regulatory body, was established in 1976. It provides a forum for all direct-selling companies in Singapore to discuss problems of common concern and to codify a high standard of business practices throughout the industry. The DSAS has adopted a Code of Conduct by which member-companies in the Association must abide by every aspect of business. Through the Code of Conduct, DSAS aims to further inculcate the spirit and practice of ethical direct-selling within its member-companies, setting examples for others to follow.

Joint Ventures/Licensing   Return to top

Foreign investors are not required to enter into joint ventures or cede management control to local interests. In Singapore, local and foreign investors are subject to the same basic laws. Apart from regulatory requirements in some sectors, the government screens investment proposals only to determine eligibility for various incentive regimes. Singapore places no restrictions on reinvestment or repatriation of earnings or capital.

Licensing is also a viable alternative in Singapore. With one of the strongest IPR protection schemes in Asia, a well-developed legal framework and an advanced manufacturing base, Singapore is an attractive location for American licensors.

Selling to the Government   Return to top

Singapore is a signatory to the WTO Agreement on Government Procurement. The U.S.-Singapore FTA provides increased access for U.S. firms to Singapore's central government procurement. U.S. firms generally find Singapore to be a receptive, open and lucrative market. The Singaporean government procurement system is considered by many American firms to be fair and transparent. However, some U.S. and local firms have expressed concerns that government-owned and government-linked companies (GLCs) may receive preferential treatment in the government procurement process. Singapore denies that it gives any preferences to GLCs or that GLCs give preferences to other GLCs. Procurement recommendations are made at the technical level and then forwarded to management for concurrence. Bidders should work closely with the project manager to determine the relative importance of decision criteria such as technical capability and price. Bidders must meet the specifications set out in the tender. Post mortem hearings or meetings for losing bidders are not required or common. Government procurement regulations are contained in Instruction Manual 3, available from the Ministry of Finance. The Singapore Government also advertises its tenders on its website at www.gebiz.gov.sg.

Distribution and Sales Channels   Return to top

Singapore's distribution and sales channels are simple, direct and open to the participation of foreign firms established in Singapore. Because of Singapore's role as a regional hub, most local distributors will also have knowledge of regional distribution rules and regulations. Most consumer goods are imported by stocking distributors who resell to retailers. Some goods are imported directly for sale in the importer's own retail outlets.

Selling Factors/Techniques   Return to top

Price, quality and service are the main selling factors in Singapore. Prospective exporters to Singapore should be aware that competition is strong and that buyers expect good after-sales service. Selling techniques vary according to the industry or the product involved, but they are comparable to the techniques used in any other sophisticated market.

Electronic Commerce   Return to top

Singapore is one of the first countries in the world to enact a law that addresses issues that arise in the context of electronic contracts and digital signatures. The Electronic Transactions Act (ETA) (Cap 88) was enacted to provide a legal foundation for electronic signatures, and to give predictability and certainty to contracts formed electronically. The Singapore ETA follows closely the UN Commission on International Trade Law (UNCITRAL) Model Law on Electronic Commerce, which sets the framework for electronic laws in many countries. The full text of the ETA can be found at the Singapore Statutes Online website (http://statutes.agc.gov.sg).

Trade Promotion and Advertising   Return to top

There are many specialized trade magazines in Singapore and scores of trade fairs that can be used to promote U.S. goods and services. The major English-language daily newspapers are the Straits Times and the Business Times. They are available at http://www.straitstimes.com and http://www.businesstimes.com.sg. The major Chinese daily is Lianhe Zaobao (http://www.zaobao.com). Leads for local advertising and promotional service agencies can be found at http://www.yellowpages.com.sg. Major trade fair organizers include Singapore Exhibition Services (http://www.sesallworld.com/), Reed Exhibition Services (http://www.reedexpo.com.sg/), Experia Events (http://www.experiaevents.com) and Koelnmesse (http://www.koelnmesse.com.sg).

Pricing   Return to top

Pricing is very competitive. Major department stores and retail chains offer fixed-price merchandise, while the smaller shops expect buyers to bargain. Hard bargaining is common in the commercial and industrial sectors as well, where buyers usually want a discount and vendors inflate their initial offers accordingly. Credit terms of 30-60-90 days are common. Buyers will often retain 10% of the sales price for major electronic equipment purchases until the vendor has installed the machine and it is performing according to specifications.

Typical Product Pricing Structures: Depending on the type of product, importer mark-ups range from 20-40%, while retail mark-ups are often more than 100%. Industrial goods are brought in by stocking distributors, who add on at least 20% before sale to end-users, or by agents whose commissions generally run about 7-10%. These mark-ups are approximate, and will vary widely, depending on the product and the contractual relationship in question.

Sales Service/Customer Support   Return to top

Good sales and customer support are vital in Singapore. The market is so price competitive that client-focused sales support or customer service can make a big difference. Singapore distributors respond well to training on new products, and if properly supported by the U.S. manufacturer will do a good job cultivating old customers and developing new ones.

Protecting Your Intellectual Property   Return to top

Several general principles are important for effective management of intellectual property ("IP") rights in Singapore. First, it is important to have an overall strategy to protect your IP. Second, IP is protected differently in Singapore than in the U.S. Third, rights must be registered and enforced in Singapore, under local laws. Your U.S. trademark and patent registrations will not protect you in Singapore. There is no such thing as an "international copyright" that will automatically protect an author's writings throughout the entire world. Protection against unauthorized use in a particular country depends, basically, on the national laws of that country. However, most countries do offer copyright protection to foreign works under certain conditions, and these conditions have been greatly simplified by international copyright treaties and conventions.

Registration of patents and trademarks is on a first-in-time, first-in-right basis, so you should consider applying for trademark and patent protection even before selling your products or services in the Singapore market. It is vital that companies understand that intellectual property is primarily a private right and that the US government generally cannot enforce rights for private individuals in Singapore. It is the responsibility of the

rights' holders to register, protect, and enforce their rights where relevant, retaining their own counsel and advisors. Companies may wish to seek advice from local attorneys or IP consultants who are experts in Singapore law. The U.S. Commercial Service can provide a list of local lawyers upon request:
http://singapore.usembassy.gov/list_of_attorneys.html

While the U.S. Government stands ready to assist, there is little we can do if the rights holders have not taken these fundamental steps necessary to securing and enforcing their IP in a timely fashion. Moreover, in many countries, rights holders who delay enforcing their rights on a mistaken belief that the USG can provide a political resolution to a legal problem may find that their rights have been eroded or abrogated due to legal doctrines such as statutes of limitations, laches, estoppel, or unreasonable delay in prosecuting a law suit. In no instance should U.S. Government advice be seen as a substitute for the obligation of a rights holder to promptly pursue its case.

It is always advisable to conduct due diligence on potential partners. Negotiate from the position of your partner and give your partner clear incentives to honor the contract. A good partner is an important ally in protecting IP rights. Consider carefully, however, whether to permit your partner to register your IP rights on your behalf. Doing so may create a risk that your partner will list itself as the IP owner and fail to transfer the rights should the partnership end. Keep an eye on your cost structure and reduce the margins (and the incentive) of would-be bad actors. Projects and sales in Singapore require constant attention. Work with legal counsel familiar with Singapore laws to create a solid contract that includes non-compete clauses, and confidentiality/non-disclosure provisions.

It is also recommended that small and medium-size companies understand the importance of working together with trade associations and organizations to support efforts to protect IP and stop counterfeiting. There are a number of these organizations, both Singapore or U.S.-based. These include:

- The U.S. Chamber and local American Chambers of Commerce
- National Association of Manufacturers (NAM)
- International Intellectual Property Alliance (IIPA)
- International Trademark Association (INTA)
- The Coalition Against Counterfeiting and Piracy
- International Anti-Counterfeiting Coalition (IACC)
- Pharmaceutical Research and Manufacturers of America (PhRMA)
- Biotechnology Industry Organization (BIO)

IP Resources
A wealth of information on protecting IP is freely available to U.S. rights holders. Some excellent resources for companies regarding intellectual property include the following:

- For information about patent, trademark, or copyright issues -- including enforcement issues in the US and other countries -- call the STOP! Hotline: **1-866-999-HALT** or visit www.STOPfakes.gov.

- For more information about registering trademarks and patents (both in the U.S. as well as in foreign countries), contact the US Patent and Trademark Office (USPTO) at: **1-800-786-9199**, or visit http://www.uspto.gov/.

- For more information about registering for copyright protection in the US, contact the US Copyright Office at: **1-202-707-5959**, or visit http://www.copyright.gov/.

- For more information about how to evaluate, protect, and enforce intellectual property rights and how these rights may be important for businesses, please visit the "Resources" section of the STOPfakes website at http://www.stopfakes.gov/resources.

- For information on obtaining and enforcing intellectual property rights and market-specific IP Toolkits visit: **www.stopfakes.gov**/businesss-tools/country-ipr-toolkits. The toolkits contain detailed information on protecting and enforcing IP in specific markets and also contain contact information for local IPR offices abroad and U.S. government officials available to assist SMEs.

- The U.S. Commerce Department has positioned IP attachés in key markets around the world. You can get contact information for the IP attaché who covers Southeast Asian region is Mr. Peter N. Fowler, Regional IP Attaché for Southeast Asia, U.S. Patent and Trademark Office, U.S. Embassy Bangkok, Room 302, GPF Witthayu Tower A, 93/1 Wireless Road, Bangkok 10330, Thailand, Tel: (662) 205-5913, Fax: (662) 255-2915, email: Peter.Fowler@trade.gov.

Due Diligence　　　　　　　　　　　　　　　　　　　　　　Return to top

Entities wanting to carry out business in Singapore must register with the Accounting and Corporate Regulatory Authority (ACRA). CS Singapore offers the International Company Profile (http://www.buyusa.gov/singapore/en/icp.html) service to American firms wishing to check the bona fides of existing or potential partners. Alternately, U.S. firms can run a check on Singapore companies by accessing the ACRA database via www.acra.gov.sg. Other credit agency includes Infocredit D&B (http://www.icdnb.com.sg).

Local Professional Services　　　　　　　　　　　　　　　Return to top

Legal Services: As of end 2013, 12 of the 114 foreign law firms in Singapore were from the United States. In December 2008, Singapore granted Qualifying Foreign Law Practice (QFLP) licenses to six foreign law firms (including two U.S. firms) to practice Singapore law, although restrictions remain in certain areas, including conveyance, criminal law, family law, and domestic litigation. In 1Q 2013, Singapore awarded another four QFLP licenses during the second round of applications, which ended in 2012 and attracted twenty three applicants. Three of these firms were U.S. companies. In total, ten QFLP licences have been issued since 2008, with five of them issued to U.S. firms. They are Gibson, Dunn & Crutcher; Jones Day; Sidley Austin; White & Case; and Latham & Watkins. Foreign law firms can otherwise provide legal services in relation to Singapore law only through a Joint Law Venture (JLV) or Formal Law Alliance (FLA) with a

Singapore law firm, in accordance with the relevant legislation. Details on the structure of the Singapore legal service can be found in http://www.lsc.gov.sg.

Accounting and Tax Services: The major international accounting firms operate in Singapore. Public accountants and at least one partner of a public accounting firm must reside in Singapore. Only public accountants who are members of the Institute of Certified Public Accountants of Singapore (http://www.icpas.org.sg) and registered with the Public Accountants Board may practice in Singapore. The Board recognizes U.S. accountants registered with the American Institute of Certified Public Accountants.

Engineering and Architectural Services: Engineering and architectural firms can be 100-percent foreign-owned. Only engineers and architects registered with the Professional Engineers Board, Singapore (http://www.peb.gov.sg) and the Board of Architects (http://www.boa.gov.sg) respectively, can practice in Singapore. All applicants (both local and foreign) must have at least four years of practical experience in engineering or architectural works, and pass an examination set by the respective Board.

Under the Architect Act, no person shall draw or prepare any architectural plan and design intended to govern the construction of any building in Singapore unless the person is a registered architect who has a valid practicing certificate issued by the Board of Architects (http://www.boa.gov.sg).

Web Resources   Return to top

http://www.buyusa.gov/singapore

http://singapore.usembassy.gov/legal_information.html

http://www.enterpriseone.gov.sg

http://www.gov.sg

http://www.gebiz.gov.sg

http://statutes.agc.gov.sg

http://www.ida.gov.sg

http://www.sg

http://www.straitstimes.com.sg

http://www.businesstimes.com.sg

http://www.zaobao.com

http://www.yellowpages.com.sg

http://www.sesallworld.com

http://www.reedexpo.com.sg

http://www.experiaevents.com

http://www.koelnmesse.com.sg

http://www.acra.gov.sg

http://www.icdnb.com.sg

http://www.StopFakes.gov

http://www.icpas.org.sg

http://www.peb.gov.sg

http://www.boa.gov.sg

http://www.lsc.gov.sg

Return to table of contents

Return to table of contents

Chapter 4: Leading Sectors for U.S. Export and Investment

Commercial Sectors

- Aircraft and Parts (AIR)
- Medical Devices
- Computer Hardware, Software & Peripherals
- Laboratory & Scientific Instruments (LAB)
- Environment Control Equipment (POL)
- Oil & Gas
- Telecommunications Equipment
- Education

Agricultural Sectors

- Fresh Fruit
- Processed Fruit & Vegetables
- Fruit & Vegetable Juices
- Fresh Vegetables

Aircraft and Parts (AIR)

Overview

Unit: USD millions

	2012	2013	2014 (estimated)	2015 (estimated)
Total Market Size	9,219	9,747	10,998	12,097
Total Local Production	6,960	7,656	8,421	9,263
Total Exports	8,549	10,001	8,338	9,172
Total Imports	10,808	12,092	10,915	12,006
Imports from the U.S.	6,494	9,633	6,627	7,290
Exchange Rate: 1 USD	1.25	1.25	1.27	1.27

Total Market Size = (Total Local Production + Total Imports) − (Total Exports)
Data Sources: Singapore Government Trade Statistics

Singapore's aerospace industry has maintained a leading position in the Asian market. Growing by an average of 12% since 1990 and generating an output of more than $6.9 billion in 2012, the aerospace industry is a key economic driver for Singapore.

As a convenient one-stop center for all aircraft maintenance needs, with a full range of MRO services and a large precision engineering suppliers base, Singapore's MRO cluster has captured about 25% of the Asia-Pacific MRO market. Going forward, besides strengthening the MRO cluster, the aerospace manufacturing and R&D segments will also be further developed. Products designed and manufactured in Singapore include engine casings, engine gears, valves, seat actuators, electrical power systems and galley equipment, among others.

Demand for business aviation is expected to grow, fuelled by Singapore's growth as a global city and an increase in air traffic movements in and out of Singapore. Works have already begun to expand Seletar Airport and enhance its infrastructure to support its development into a leading business aviation airport. Upon completion in 2018, the upgraded Seletar Airport will greatly enhance its services to the business and commercial aviation community.

Air traffic growth for the Asia-Pacific region is expected to stay ahead of the global average, underpinned by demand in fast growing China and India. Singapore is particularly well-equipped to capture the demand from aviation-related services from this market given its MRO hub status, which will translate into greater opportunities for American suppliers to sell to this lucrative market.

Best Products/Services

The boom in low-cost travel and a growing web of open-skies agreements are expected to power long-term growth for Asian airlines in the years ahead. As an aerospace hub in the Asia Pacific, Singapore is most definitely going to reap the benefits of this upturn.

In addition to supplying to all aspects of the MRO business, Singapore will see new growth opportunities in the areas of business aviation, regional training, and asset management.

Opportunities   Return to top

Singapore is constantly developing its aerospace industry, particularly in its MRO sector. This will undoubtedly provide greater opportunities in Singapore for MRO activities to grow and so are the supply of aircraft parts and systems.

Web Resources   Return to top

Trade Show

Singapore Air Show 2016
February 16-21, 2016
http://www.singaporeairshow.com.sg

Singapore Government Offices

Singapore Economic Development Board
http://www.sedb.com.sg

Civil Aviation Authority of Singapore
http://www.caas.gov.sg

Defense Science & Technology Agency
http://www.dsta.gov.sg

U.S. Commercial Service, Singapore Contact
Ng Haw Cheng, Commercial Specialist
Email: Hawcheng.Ng@trade.gov

Medical Devices

Overview   Return to top

Unit: USD millions

	2012	2013	2014 (estimated)	2015 (estimated)
Total Market Size	2740	2356	2186	2295
Total Local Production	8348	8193	8468	8891
Total Exports	15372	15278	16536	17363
Total Imports	9764	9441	10254	10767
Imports from the U.S.	2972	3634	4071	4276
Exchange Rate: 1 USD	1.25	1.25	1.27	1.27

Total Market Size = (Total Local Production + Total Imports) – (Total Exports)
Data Sources: Singapore Government Trade Statistics

According to the World Health Organization (WHO), Singapore's healthcare system ranks sixth globally and offers the 4th best healthcare infrastructure in the world. It also serves as the healthcare and medical hub of the region and is arguably Asia's best healthcare system. The Joint Commission International (JCI) has accredited 11 Singapore hospitals and three medical centers. Each year, it draws over 350,000 patients with its high-quality healthcare. The government spends approximately 4% of GDP annually on healthcare and there are long run plans to raise this to 8% of GDP. Healthcare spending is expected to reach $6.2 billion in 2015. The government's projected healthcare spending is expected to triple to $9.45 billion a year by 2020, up from $3.2 billion in 2011. A survey by Swiss Re, a Swiss based insurance provider, in 2013 found that Singaporeans are among the best prepared for future health expenses among five countries in Asia. It reported that 74% of working adults are prepared for post-retirement health expenditures, which puts Singapore higher than Hong Kong, China, Japan and South Korea.

In 2013, imports of medical equipment and supplies to Singapore decreased marginally over the previous year. This can be attributed to a sharper increase in imports the previous year due to increased spending associated with the establishment of new hospitals and healthcare facilities. U.S. imports, however, grew by 22% over the previous year and accounted for 38.5% of market share, a 7% increase in market share over 2012.

Based on available trade figures for 2012 and 2013, U.S. exports of medical equipment to Singapore will continue to be healthy and positive in 2014. This is attributed primarily to the nature of the healthcare industry as well as the premium and goodwill that American brands enjoy in this sector. As regional economies enjoy higher economic growth and improvements in healthcare standards and delivery, transshipments through Singapore will increase. At present, approximately 40% of products imported into Singapore are subsequently re-exported.

Medical devices are regulated under the Health Products Act and Health Products (Medical Devices) regulations. Singapore's Health Sciences Authority (HSA) oversees the system of statutory control aimed to safeguard the quality, safety and efficacy of medical devices available in Singapore. Almost all medical devices are regulated. Class A medical devices supplied in a non-sterile state are exempted, however, Class A sterile, Class B, C and D medical devices are subject to product registration requirements. Classification rules are adopted from the guidance developed by the Global Harmonization Task Force (GHTF).

Sub-Sector Best Prospects   Return to top

Based on available data, the Ministry of Health was allocated a total of $3.36 billion in 2011 to achieve its mission of delivering affordable healthcare and ensuring good medical outcomes, reducing illness and promoting good health, and ensuring that the country is resilient against communicable disease threats and civil emergencies. Two years ago, the Singapore government announced a $5.6 billion budget that addresses infrastructure concerns in the short and long term as well as healthcare provision and subsidies for the poor. The three key areas of focus will be healthcare infrastructure, healthcare delivery and managing the associated costs and issues relating to an aging population. This budget also includes larger subsidies for surgical implants, the treatment and management of chronic diseases, as well as funding programs to promote healthy lifestyle and active-aging programs. As a result, U.S. exporters of medical devices, preventive and health screening products, and disease management solutions would be able to benefit.

The Singapore government also remains committed to ensuring that the national healthcare system keeps pace with global medical advancements. To keep up with advances in biomedical science and encourage the development of new clinical treatments for Singaporeans, the Ministry of Health, in partnership with A*STAR (Agency for Science, Technology & Research) and several other governmental bodies, will invest $53 million in clinical and translational research. Another $10.6 million has been set aside for the development of new clinical services. The aim is to augment Singapore's medical capabilities in the public healthcare system and position Singapore as the premier regional medical services hub. U.S. exporters who are able to provide cutting-edge technology, laboratory and testing equipment and services for the healthcare and research communities will find Singapore a lucrative market.

Within the next twenty years, Singapore will experience what is being called 'hyper-aging.' Over a quarter of the population will be 65 years and older by 2030. As such, more facilities for the elderly, such as nursing homes and rehabilitation centers, need to be built. The number of beds in community hospitals and nursing homes will increase substantially over the next few years and six new nursing homes are planned to be operational by 2015. U.S. firms specializing in elder-care products and services will find a robust and growing market in Singapore.

Opportunities   Return to top

According to Frost & Sullivan, by 2015, Asia Pacific's healthcare market is expected to reach close to 33% of the global healthcare market and estimated to be valued at $521 billion with trends in the medical device industry in Asia mainly centered on imaging, cardiovascular and healthcare IT. A key driver for the Southeast Asian region is the impending liberalization of the services sector by 2015 under the ASEAN agreement. A 2012 study by Deloitte Centre for Health Solutions indicates that Southeast Asia has the highest private health expenditure of any region in the world, at 63.1% of total health expenditures. This has led to increased private-public sector collaboration in Singapore, Malaysia and Thailand.

Singapore is renowned for its role as a healthcare hub for the region, treating patients from neighboring Malaysia, Brunei, Indonesia, Thailand, Philippines and more recently, from the Americas, Europe and the Asia Pacific.

Government hospitals account for 80% of all hospital beds in Singapore. It is projected that by 2015, there will be a total of 12,900 hospital beds. Three quarters or 9,700 will come from the public sector with the private sector accounting for the rest. Under Healthcare 2020, over 4000 new public hospital and community hospital beds will be added by 2020.

Demand for medical equipment comes from public and private hospitals and clinics. The Health Ministry is the largest consumer, accounting for nearly 70% of local demand. All public and the majority of private sector hospitals are Joint Commission International (JCI) accredited. Parkway Healthcare, the largest private sector healthcare provider in Singapore, is also a significant buyer of medical equipment. More than 80% of local demand is met through imports and there is a premium placed on American-made products. U.S. manufacturers with innovative products will find Singapore a good market place.

In the medium term, six new public hospitals and up to 12 more polyclinics will be built by 2030 to ensure that Singapore has adequate healthcare coverage. There are also plans to build 12 new and replacement nursing homes by 2016, bringing the total to 25 by 2020. Given that the world is facing infectious disease threats due to more global travel and increased connectivity, a new 300-bed hospital for infectious disease will be built. It is expected to be ready by 2018. In addition, a new 12-storey, $135 million National Heart Center building, three times larger than the size of the existing one, will be built at the Singapore General Hospital.

One-third of the private sector's patient mix is from overseas. Recognizing the growth potential of the foreign patient sector, various private sector healthcare groups have embarked on renovations and expansion programs. Among them, the Parkway and Raffles groups over the last two years have appropriated between $61.5 million and $345 million to build, expand and upgrade their healthcare facilities.

Web Resources   Return to top

Trade Shows

Medical Fair Asia 2014
September 9-11, 2014
http://www.medicalfair-asia.com

International Dental Exhibition & Meeting 2016 (IDEM)
April 8-10, 2016
http://www.idem-singapore.com/

Singapore Government Offices

Singapore Ministry of Health (MOH)
http://www.moh.gov.sg

Health Sciences Authority (HSA)
http://www.hsa.gov.sg

Health Promotion Board (HPB)
http://www.hpb.gov.sg

Agency for Integrated Care (AIC)
http://www.aic.sg/

Singapore Economic Development Board (SEDB)
http://www.edb.gov.sg

U.S. Commercial Service, Singapore Contact

Luanne Theseira, Commercial Specialist
Email: Luanne.Theseira@trade.gov

Computer Hardware, Software & Peripherals

Overview   Return to top

Unit: USD millions

	2012	2013	2014 (estimated)	2015 (estimated)
Total Market Size	5395	4558	3470	3500
Total Local Production	14310	11878	9980	10050
Total Exports	23180	20356	18900	18950
Total Imports	14265	13036	12390	12400
Imports from the U.S.	1344	1201	1300	1400
Exchange Rate: 1 USD	1.25	1.25	1.27	1.27

Total Market Size = (Total Local Production + Total Imports) – (Total Exports)
Data Sources: estimates based on Singapore Government Trade Statistics

According to the 13th edition of the Global Information Technology report published by Business School Insead, "Singapore has become one of the most knowledge-intensive economies globally, and is an infocomm technology-genenration powerhouse." It ranked Singapore second in using infocomm technology to improve economic productivity and social development. Singapore also topped the 2013 Waseda University World e-Government Ranking and was ranked second in the World Economic Forum's Global IT Report 2013.

Many top IT companies have made Singapore a key node in their global network, a strong testament to the country's strategic position as a global info-communications hub. With the successful rollout of its 10 year IT Master Plan called IN2015, the Singapore government is now seeking to develop a Master Plan for the Infocomm and media (ICM) sectors for the next 10 years. Its goal is to establish Singapore as a Smart Nation that leads the world in tapping the potential of ICM that nurtures innovative talent and enterprises and contribute to a better quality of life for its people as well as a sustainable and quality growth for the country.

Latest available data showed that computer usage amongst all enterprises increased by 1% to 84% in 2012. Internet usage increased to 84% while 80% of enterprises used broadband access. Data on info-communications usage by individuals, household and enterprises can be found at http://www.ida.gov.sg/Infocomm-Landscape/Facts-and-Figures.aspx

Sub-Sector Best Prospects   Return to top

The Singapore Government is not only a major catalyst for promoting the use of information technology in the country but is also a major user of IT products and services. Best prospects include government projects, security solutions, business analytics, data centers and cloud computing, and solutions in the following industries:

healthcare, education, trade & logistics, tourism hospitality and retail, and financial services.

Opportunities Return to top

The Singapore government invested $960 million (S$1.2 billion) in information technology projects in FY2013 and announced it will invest the same amount in FY2014 (April 2014-March 2015). U.S. companies interested in doing business with the Singapore government should register with GeBIZ (http://www.gebiz.gov.sg/), the Singapore government's one-stop e-procurement portal where all the public sector's invitations for quotations and tenders are posted. Both local and foreign suppliers are able to search for government procurement opportunities, download tender documents, and submit their bids online.

The Infocomm Development Authority (IDA) functions as the government's Chief Information Officer and is responsible for master-planning, project-managing and implementing various infocomm systems and capabilities for the government. The IDA oversees IT standards, policies, guidelines and procedures for the Government, and manages the infocomm security of critical infocomm infrastructure. In addition, the IDA promotes the adoption of infocomm technology as a key enabler to enhance Singapore's economic competitiveness. It works with both public and private organizations to spearhead the strategic use of infocomm in the various industry sectors. U.S. companies interested in partnering with the IDA on collaboration opportunities should review http://www.ida.gov.sg/Collaboration-and-Initiatives/Collaboration-Opportunities.

Web Resources Return to top

Trade Shows

Enterprise IT 2015
June 16-19, 2015

http://www.goto-enterpriseit.com/

Key websites

http://www.ida.gov.sg

http://www.sitf.org.sg

http://export.gov/mrktresearch/index.asp

U.S. Commercial Service, Singapore Contact

Ms. CHIA Swee Hoon, Senior Commercial Specialist
Email: SweeHoon.Chia@trade.gov

Laboratory & Scientific Instruments (LAB)

Overview　　　　　　　　　　　　　　　　　　　　　　　　Return to top

Unit: USD millions

	2012	2013	2014 (estimated)	2015 (estimated)
Total Market Size	6401	6499	5895	5775
Total Local Production	10085	10524	10195	10297
Total Exports	15489	16237	16986	17665
Total Imports	11805	12212	12686	13143
Imports from the U.S.	4200	4299	4224	4308
Exchange Rate: 1 USD	1.25	1.25	1.27	1.27

Total Market Size = (Total Local Production + Total Imports) – (Total Exports)
Data Sources: Singapore Government Trade Statistics

Singapore's Research, Innovation & Enterprise (RIE) 2015 plan targets to develop Singapore into one of the world's leading research-intensive, innovative and entrepreneurial economies. Developing deep R&D capabilities continues to remain a key priority. Under this plan, Singapore plans on spending 3.5% of GDP on R&D. According to A*STAR's (Agency for Science, Technology & Research) latest R&D survey, public expenditure on R&D has steadily increased over the past ten years, reaching $2.25 billion in 2012 or 0.8% of GDP while R&D by local private companies increased by $144 million to $1.04 billion.

Five years ago, the government injected approximately $29 million into developing medical technology and devices that could be brought to market faster. In 2000, when Singapore began its push into the biomedical sciences, the medical technology industry was worth $1.2 billion. By 2008, its manufacturing output was worth $2.3 billion and it is expected that by 2015, it will hit $4 billion. Eleven years into Singapore's biomedical sciences push, the sector has also grown into a sizeable stable of almost 300 companies and businesses including over 30 global medical technology companies that have set up commercial-scale manufacturing plants in Singapore.

The United States continues to dominate in the area of laboratory and scientific equipment and accounts for approximately 35% of total imports. Total imports from the U.S. marginally increased by 2.4% in 2013. This corresponds with a 3.4% increase in total overall imports. There is a strong preference for American manufactured products, particularly in the field of laboratory equipment and scientific instrumentation. With Singapore's strong and keen focus across a broad spectrum of industry, such as precision engineering, chemicals, and biomedical sciences to name a few, exports of American laboratory and scientific equipment is expected to remain constant.

Sub-Sector Best Prospects　　　　　　　　　　　　　　　　Return to top

The industry clusters that support the demand for laboratory and scientific equipment are the biomedical sciences, clean technologies (which encompasses environmental and water technologies), microelectronics, petrochemicals, specialty chemicals, marine and offshore engineering, interactive and digital media, data storage, and institutional R&D laboratories. Several of these key sectors attracted substantial new investment.

The National Research Council, a Singapore government initiative, provides a national framework for strategic research and development efforts. The broad areas of focus are the biomedical sciences, translational and clinical research, energy, environmental and water technologies, as well as interactive and digital media. The Energy Innovation Challenge Directorate (EICD) was established in 2011 to catalyze significant changes in Singapore's energy landscape. Their goal is to harness Singapore's vibrant R&D base to develop innovative solutions to meet the objectives of competitiveness, energy security and environmental sustainability.

In the area of biomedical sciences, more than 7000 researchers carry out research and development for more than 50 companies, universities and private and public sector research institutes. More than $1.23 billion is spent on biomedical R&D annually. The global medical technology industry is projected to exceed $300 billion by 2017 with a significant contribution to this expansion coming from the Asia-Pacific market.

Opportunities   Return to top

Looking ahead, Singapore has committed $13.3 billion in continued support of research, innovation and enterprise activities through 2015. Of this, $3 billion is dedicated to existing biomedical R&D infrastructure, integrating multi-disciplinary research and translating basic science into tangible outcomes. Considerable resources are being poured into six key research areas, specifically molecular, cellular and developmental biology, cancer genetics, stem cells and regenerative medicines, immunology and infectious disease, metabolic medicine, and biomedical engineering. Many global companies and Asian enterprises have significant operations in Singapore, including eight of the world's top ten pharmaceutical companies, all of the top ten medical technology companies, as well as several global skincare and personal care companies. U.S. firms include GE Healthcare, Johnson & Johnson, Amgen, Merck, Baxter, BD and Procter & Gamble.

Recognizing that Asia is home to half of the world's population, Singapore is betting on clean technologies as a strategic economic growth area. To achieve this, Singapore has allocated approximately $580 million to develop five key areas for clean technologies. These are research and development, manpower development, grooming Singapore-based enterprises, branding Singapore's clean technology industry internationally, and developing a vibrant cleantech eco-system. There are more than 70 water companies present in Singapore and these include U.S. firms like GE Water and Black & Veach.

Web Resources   Return to top

Trade Shows

BioPharma Asia Convention 2015
March 23-26, 2015

http://www.terrapinn.com/exhibition/bio-asia/index.stm

MEDLAB Asia 2015
March 18-20, 2015
http://www.medlabasia.com/

Singapore Government Offices

A*STAR (Agency for Science, Technology & Research)
http://www.a-star.edu.sg

Singapore Economic Development Board (SEDB)
http://www.edb.gov.sg

U.S. Commercial Service, Singapore Contact

Luanne Theseira, Commercial Specialist
Email: Luanne.Theseira@trade.gov

Environment Control Equipment (POL)

Overview Return to top

Unit: USD millions

	2012	2013	2014 (estimated)	2015 (estimated)
Total Market Size	19,557	16,697	17,094	17,620
Total Local Production	17,377	17,898	18,435	18,988
Total Exports	10,234	11,609	11,957	12,196
Total Imports	12,414	10,408	10,616	10,828
Imports from the U.S.	2,146	2,049	2,090	2,131
Exchange Rate: 1 USD	1.25	1.25	1.27	1.27

Total Market Size = (Total Local Production + Total Imports) – (Total Exports)
Data Sources: Singapore Government Trade Statistics; Statistics are unofficial estimates

The harsh realities of climate change and pollution have spurred on the momentum of the Government of Singapore and many companies here to find and adopt environmentally-friendly services and solutions for implementation. In particular, Singapore has placed great emphasis in developing the clean technology sector which includes the fields of clean energy, and environment and water.

A holistic blueprint is already in place to grow the clean energy industry with US$280 million of public funds. Its initiatives include the US$40 million Clean Energy Research Program (CERP) set up to support R&D efforts as well as a US$50 million MND Research Fund for the Built Environment managed by the Building and Construction Authority.

The water industry has also been identified as a key growth sector for Singapore's economy. The industry is one that Singapore has a vested interest in, given its national emphasis on water management. An additional US$264 million has been committed to develop R&D and manpower capabilities with the aim of positioning Singapore as a Global Hydrohub – an international center to develop and provide water technologies and solutions. The water industry is expected to triple its value-added to the Singapore economy to US$1.36 billion by 2015.

Best Products/Services Return to top

Singapore's Green Plan 2012 (SGP 2012) incorporates programs for reduction of waste volumes through waste minimization and recycling; reduction of the amount of land for sewage treatment; stricter emission standards, and tougher vehicular emission controls. The Singapore Government has announced it will upgrade and build environmental infrastructure projects over the next ten years. Related products from the U.S. will have good market prospects, given that imports of environmental products from the U.S. account for about 20% of the total imports.

Opportunities   Return to top

Water technologies also offer great opportunities in Singapore. The water industry in Singapore is becoming more liberalized. The national water agency, the Public Utilities Board (PUB), has opened its doors to private companies that want to test-bed projects using its infrastructure. PUB also offers contracts to private companies to design, build and operate water plants. U.S. companies are encouraged to participate in future tenders offered by the PUB. American manufacturers could also supply their equipment to the successful prime contractors of PUB projects. Areas of particular interest include filtering and purifying machinery and apparatus, technologies involving wastewater recycling and treatment, and modular wastewater treatment systems.

Web Resources   Return to top

Trade Show

Singapore International Water Week
July, 2016
http://www.siww.com.sg

WasteMET Asia
July, 2016
http://www.wastemetasia.sg

World Cities Summit
July, 2016
http://www.worldcitiessummit.com.sg

Singapore Government Offices

Ministry of the Environment & Water Resources
http://www.mewr.gov.sg

National Environment Agency
http://www.nea.gov.sg

Public Utilities Board
http://www.pub.gov.sg

U.S. Commercial Service, Singapore Contact

Ng Haw Cheng, Commercial Specialist
Email: Hawcheng.Ng@trade.gov

Oil & Gas

Overview Return to top

Unit: USD millions

	2012	2013	2014 (estimated)	2015 (estimated)
Total Market Size	109,256	111,413	118,000	123,000
Total Local Production	75,165	75,676	80,000	88,000
Total Exports	105,615	98,514	100,000	105,000
Total Imports	139,706	134,251	138,000	140,000
Imports from the U.S.	4,606	4,681	5,500	5,500
Exchange Rate: 1 USD	1.25	1.25	1.27	1.27

Total Market Size = (Total Local Production + Total Imports) – (Total Exports)
Data Sources: Singapore Government Trade Statistics

Singapore has become one of the most important shipping centers in Asia and is one of the world's top five oil trading and refining hubs. In addition, Singapore is the market leader for floating production, storage and offloading (FPSOs) conversions and jack-up rigs. Underground caverns for oil storage and a liquid natural gas (LNG) terminal are also being expanded in phases to enhance Singapore's position as the premier regional center for the oil & gas industry. Despite global economic uncertainty and fluctuating oil prices, the growth and imports are expected to be promising over the next 12 months due to increase oil & gas exploration.

Sub-Sector Best Prospects Return to top

Singapore offers many opportunities for American companies including:

- Supply of equipment for upstream and downstream oil and gas, shipbuilding, marine, mechanical and electrical construction, oxidation additives and various control systems

- Oilfield equipment that includes instrumentation such as drilling information systems, drilling monitors, mud logging units, mud monitoring systems, torque gauges, pressure gauges, weight indicators, deadline anchors, valves / actuators, performance testing and design control system

- Supply of tubular products such as casings, tubing, carbon steel line pipes, drill pipes, heavy wall pipes, drill collars, drill stem accessories and mechanical alloy steel tubes

Opportunities Return to top

Singapore is often listed as the leading oil trading hub in Asia (third in the world after New York and London) and amongst the world's top five oil refining centers. It has a refining capacity of nearly double its rate of petroleum products consumption. It is also a world leader in the construction of exploration and production platforms and holds the No. 1 position, with more than 50 percent market share for FPSOs conversions as well as for jack-up rigs.

Engineering, procurement and construction of the $700 million LNG terminal was awarded in late 2009 to a Korean consortium led by Samsung. The first phase was completed in 2013 with the arrival of the first shipment of LNG from Qatar. Future expansion work (including a second LNG terminal) costing more than $500 million is already being planned as Singapore aims to be a future hub for natural gas trading and trans-shipment in Asia. Once all phases are completed by 2017, the first terminal will be able to handle nine million metric tons per year.

The construction of Very Large Floating Structures (VLFS) for storage of oil and petroleum products is also being explored since land is scarce. Feasibility studies are underway to determine the impact of sea currents and metocean conditions according to recent press reports. To be economical, the minimum storage capacity of a VLFS would be 300,000 cubic meters or equivalent to that of a very large crude carrier. It is estimated that it would cost $150 million or more – the decision to move forward will be made by end 2014 with the issue of a tender (engineering, procurement and construction) but actual construction will commence in 2015 at the earliest.

Web Resources   Return to top

Trade Shows

OSEA 2014
December 2-5, 2014
http://www.osea-asia.com

Singapore Government Offices

Singapore Economic Development Board (SEDB)
http://www.edb.gov.sg

U.S. Commercial Service, Singapore Contact

CHAN Y K, Commercial Specialist
E-mail: yiukei.chan@trade.gov

Telecommunications Equipment

Overview   Return to top

Unit: USD millions

	2012	2013	2014 (estimated)	2015 (estimated)
Total Market Size	4460	2927	1230	1240
Total Local Production	3047	2292	1930	1950
Total Exports	10246	10388	9600	9700
Total Imports	11658	11023	8900	8990
Imports from the U.S.	1171	996	800	800
Exchange Rate: 1 USD	1.25	1.25	1.27	1.27

Total Market Size = (Total Local Production + Total Imports) – (Total Exports)
Data Sources: estimates based on Singapore Government Trade Statistics

Telecommunications and Internet facilities in Singapore are state-of-the-art, providing high-quality communications with the rest of the world. For mobile phone users, third generation (3G) networks and services were rolled out in early 2005. Since 2011, the telecom operators progressively launched 4G or long term evolution (LTE) mobile networks.

There are three main mobile telephony providers, 13 mobile virtual network operators or MVNOs and 79 Internet Services Providers in Singapore. The mobile penetration rate was 156.3% in March 2014. Household residential wired broadband penetration rate was 105.6% while wireless broadband penetration rate was 184.8%. Internet users can register for an account and go online for free with Wireless@SG, a wireless broadband service that offers access speeds of up to 2Mbp at Wi-Fi hot spots island-wide in public places such as shopping malls, town centers and the business district.
http://www.ida.gov.sg/Infocomm-Landscape/Infrastructure/Wireless

More than 95% of homes and offices in Singapore have access to the new, ultra high speed, all-fiber Next Generation Nationwide Broadband Network (Next Gen NBN) offering broadband speeds of up to 1 Gbps. Besides a nationwide broadband network infrastructure, Singapore is well connected by multiple satellite and submarine cable systems with more than 119.4 terabits per second (Tbps) of potential capacity supporting international and regional telecoms connectivity. It has more than 2.18 terabits per second (Tbps) of international internet bandwidth connectivity to economies such as the US, China, Japan, India, as well as some countries in Europe and ASEAN. Telecom statistics can be found at:
http://www.ida.gov.sg/Infocomm-Landscape/Facts-and-Figures/Telecommunications/Statistics-on-Telecom-Services.aspx

Sub-Sector Best Prospects   Return to top

Singapore is dependent on imports and U.S. products are traditionally well received here. There are excellent opportunities to sell new applications and solutions to Singapore, as it is traditionally an early adopter of such innovations. The country serves as a major distribution center for companies interested in selling to the region. More than 70% of telecommunications goods imported into Singapore are re-exported for third country consumption. Best prospects include equipment, content, software and technologies for broadband, wireless broadband, and 4G.

Opportunities   Return to top

The Infocomm Development Authority (IDA) works with both public and private organizations to spearhead the strategic use of infocomm in various industry sectors. U.S. companies interested in partnering with the IDA can access more information here:

http://www.ida.gov.sg/Collaboration-and-Initiatives/Collaboration-Opportunities
http://www.ida.gov.sg/Collaboration-and-Initiatives/Initiatives

There are also good opportunities for U.S. companies to sell solutions to Singapore's telecom service operators as they seek to offer new applications for new broadband infrastructure and mobile services. The three largest telecom service providers in Singapore are Singapore Telecommunications (SingTel), StarHub, and M1; all three are investing in infrastructure to support their new offerings.

Web Resources   Return to top

Trade Show

CommunicAsia/BroadcastAsia 2015, June 16-19, 2015
http://www.communicasia.com
http://www.broadcast-asia.com

Key websites

http://www.ida.gov.sg

http://www.sitf.org.sg/

http://www.atis.org.sg

http://export.gov/mrktresearch/index.asp

U.S. Commercial Service, Singapore Contact

Ms. CHIA Swee Hoon, Senior Commercial Specialist
Email: SweeHoon.Chia@trade.gov

Education

Overview   Return to top

Unit: USD thousands

	Sep 2007	Sep 2008	Sep 2009	Sep 2010	Sep 2011	Sep 2012	Sep 2013	Sep 2014	Sep 2015
Number of visas issued to Singaporeans	2363	2560	2676	2934	2952	3179	3310	3500	3700
% increase / decrease from previous year	0	8.3	4.5	10	0.6	7.68	4	5.7	5.7
Total visas issued including foreign students	3804	4349	4454	4870	4789	5112	5194	5300	5500
% increase / decrease from previous year	11.3	14.3	2.4	9	-1.66	-6.74	1.6	2	3.8

Figures for 2014-15 are estimated only.

Singapore emphasizes, supports and values higher education as well as human resource development and skills upgrading. Many government agencies and private sector companies also offer full scholarships for top students to pursue their undergraduate and graduate studies in foreign universities, including in the United States. More and more adult workers are also encouraged to upgrade themselves to be more knowledgeable in a globalized economy.

Sub-Sector Best Prospects   Return to top

There are currently close to 5,000 Singaporeans (excluding exchange students) pursuing tertiary education in the United States; two-thirds are undergraduates and a third are graduate students.

U.S. universities and colleges will find a receptive market in Singapore, provided they are willing to invest in long-term branding / marketing with accredited programs in disciplines that offer strong career growth and high income potential. The following degree courses are becoming increasingly important and are expected to see increased demand from Singaporean and third-country students studying in Singapore.

- Life Sciences / Healthcare
- Supply Chain Logistics
- Hospitality & Tourism
- Media & Animation
- Sports Science & Medicine
- Wealth Management / Financial Planning

Opportunities   Return to top

Singapore government is developing the country into the "global schoolhouse" for Asia. The education system is well known for its quality, which is why there is a strong demand from students in the region to study here. American universities, in addition to recruiting full-time students (both local and overseas) to study in the United States, may want to consider offering their external degree and executive education programs in Singapore to Singaporeans as well as international executives working in the region. However, a Private Education Bill passed in November 2009 effectively established a non-tariff trade barrier for certain education institutions. The bill adversely affected the ability of some U.S. universities to offer external degree programs and has implications for other American education providers seeking to offer degree, diploma or certificate courses in Singapore.

Simply having proper recognition and/or accreditation in the foreign institution's own country is only a starting point for approval for a foreign institution seeking to offer programs or courses in Singapore. In addition to meeting Singapore's standards, "national ranking" appears to be a key criterion for approval. The Council for Private Education was set up to regulate this new Bill and by end of 2014, they are expected to complete the evaluation of all existing private education institutions (PEIs) and foreign degree programs that are offered in Singapore. According to industry sources, the number of PEIs has been reduced to a third of what it used to be.

In addition to Singaporeans, U.S. universities and colleges should also consider the large number of foreign students studying at the high school and university levels in Singapore especially since more than 90,000 foreign students study in Singapore. Many foreign universities have established a presence in Singapore either on their own or in collaboration with a local institution to offer partial or full degree programs. Singaporean students find programs that allow them to complete at least part of their course work in Singapore a very attractive and financially viable alternative to completing their studies entirely in the United States.

Web Resources   Return to top

Trade Shows

USEIC U.S. Education Fairs
http://www.useic.org

Linden Education Fairs
http://www.lindentours.com

Singapore Government Offices

Council for Private Education
http://www.cpe.gov.sg

Ministry of Education
http://www.moe.gov.sg

U.S. Commercial Service, Singapore Contact

CHAN Y K, Commercial Specialist
E-mail: yiukei.chan@trade.gov

Agricultural Sectors

Fresh Fruit

Overview

Unit: USD thousands

	2012	2013	2014 (estimated)	2015 (estimated)
Total Market Size	393220	423002	451359	481587
Total Local Production	0	0	0	0
Total Exports	45387	62678	68319	74468
Total Imports	438607	485680	519678	556055
Imports from the U.S.	83227	89522	96415	103839
Exchange Rate: 1 USD	1.25	1.25	1.27	1.27

Total Market Size = (Total Local Production + Total Imports) – (Total Exports)
Data Sources: Global Trade Atlas

Fresh Fruit Best Prospects

Singapore as a major trading hub in Southeast Asia is well placed to source a wide range of fruit from all over the world. In addition, Singapore with one of the highest per capita incomes in the world and with its well-traveled population is prepared to try products from different suppliers. Quality rather than price drives the domestic market for imported fruit. This is clearly evidenced by the fact that air flown highly perishable fruit are able to command premium prices from the middle income and upper middle income segments. Major temperate fruit exporters like Australia, New Zealand, South Africa, EU, China and the United States dominate the market for temperate fruit. The United States is the leading suppliers for oranges, table grapes, cherries, peaches and plums. With the exception of China, the United States does not have any serious competition from other exporters in the Northern Hemisphere.

Opportunities

Singapore consumers have a high regard for the quality of U.S. fresh produce. Prices of U.S. fruit are extremely competitive. Retail outlets from large supermarket chains to small individual fruit stalls provide the nation-wide distribution for U.S. fruit. In addition, U.S. exporters who are prepared to promote new fruit varieties, invest in attractive packaging and consumer educational materials will reap higher sales returns.

Processed Fruit & Vegetables

Overview   Return to top

Unit: USD thousands

	2013	2014	2015 (estimated)	2016 (estimated)
Total Market Size	221918	257938	282541	307418
Total Local Production	0	0	0	0
Total Exports	108627	107178	113609	120425
Total Imports	330545	365116	396150	427843
Imports from the U.S.	67261	76835	86315	97536
Exchange Rate: 1 USD	1.25	1.25	1.27	1.27

Total Market Size = (Total Local Production + Total Imports) – (Total Exports)
Data Sources: Global Trade Atlas

Processed Fruit & Vegetables Best Prospects   Return to top

Greater numbers in tourist arrivals and rising consumer incomes have driven up the imports of processed fruit and vegetables. Imports have increased by more than 8 percent in 2013 compared to the previous year. The rise in imports has also reflected the increase in demand in re-exports to the neighboring ASEAN markets. With the overall improvement in the regional economies, the Singapore import market for processed fruit and vegetables has recorded remarkable annual growth rates ranging between 8-12 per during the period 2012-2013. The United States has maintained its market share of close to one fifth of the total imports due to local consumer preference for quality products.

Opportunities   Return to top

Over the last five years, rising tourist arrivals and the proliferation of new restaurants have provided the market opportunities for processed fruit and vegetables. With rising wage costs and the difficulty of hiring service and kitchen help, processed fruit and vegetables are a boon to the service industry. As more and more women participate in the labor force, working couples do not have very much time to prepare their daily meals. Processed fruit and vegetables are ready meal solutions to busy households who are not prepared to spend too much time in the kitchen after a long and busy day in office.

Fruit & Vegetable Juices

Overview

Unit: USD thousands

	2012	2013	2014 (estimated)	2015 (estimated)
Total Market Size	36840	33214	34029	34434
Total Local Production	0	0	0	0
Total Exports	37192	47354	53984	61541
Total Imports	74032	80568	88013	95975
Imports from the U.S.	15140	14120	15390	16776
Exchange Rate: 1 USD	1.25	1.25	1.27	1.27

Total Market Size = (Total Local Production + Total Imports) – (Total Exports)
Data Sources: Global Trade Atlas

Fruit & Vegetable Juices Best Prospects

With the general improvement of the Singapore economy and the rise in consumer incomes, total imports of fruit and vegetable juices similarly grew by over 8 percent in 2013. The improvement in demand for fruit and vegetable juices may be attributed to the rise in consumer spending in the retail and restaurant industry. U.S. brands continue to have a significant market share of close to 18 percent primarily due to consumer preference for quality products and established brands. The presence of lower priced fruit and vegetable juices from neighboring countries have not eroded U.S. market share as Singapore consumers are rather discerning in food purchasing preferences.

Opportunities

Singapore consumers are regular consumers of fruit and vegetable juices. Retail outlets that provide ready packed or freshly squeezed fruit and vegetable juices are often very well patronized. The Singapore consumers respond very well to new juice blends and varieties as well as attractive packaging. Some of the local fruit juice stalls retail freshly squeezed juices in very attractive bottles which are often reused by consumers. Educational materials on consumer health distributed along with the packed products are very good sales tools to for the promotion of new to the market products.

Fresh Vegetables

Overview   Return to top

Unit: USD thousands

	2012	2013	2014 (estimated)	2015 (estimated)
Total Market Size	373050	407766	440949	476820
Total Local Production	0	0	0	0
Total Exports	20892	28077	29761	31547
Total Imports	393942	435843	470710	508367
Imports from the U.S.	16403	17387	18430	19536
Exchange Rate: 1 USD	1.25	1.25	1.27	1.27

Total Market Size = (Total Local Production + Total Imports) – (Total Exports)
Data Sources: Global Trade Atlas

Fresh Vegetables Best Prospects   Return to top

The positive economic turnaround in 2013 coupled with the rising consumer incomes in the last decade have created a robust consumer market in Singapore as more and more households are prepared to spend a larger percentage of their disposable incomes on better quality fresh produce especially imported produce from temperate climatic countries. In addition as Singaporeans are well-traveled, have studied or have worked abroad, they are increasingly more conversant with the preparation of western cuisines using temperate climatic vegetables.

Opportunities   Return to top

The proliferation in the number of western style restaurants supported by the larger numbers of professionals and executive employees working in Singapore have contributed to the rapid growth rates for imported vegetables from the temperate climatic areas. Most of the supermarket chains have also gone upscale in their offering of a wider range of imported vegetables. It is anticipated that the growth of imported western type vegetables will continue to grow between 8-12 percent per annum over the next five years.

The rising number of tourist arrivals in recent years together with the large numbers of expatriate workers from EU, Japan and the United States has led to an increase in the demand for consumption of imported vegetables from Australia, New Zealand, United States and the EU.

Also, in the last decade, more and more Singaporeans have traveled to a wide number of countries and have experienced different cuisines and food products and as a result are extremely familiar with the consumption of western climatic vegetables.

Return to table of contents

Return to table of contents

Chapter 5: Trade Regulations, Customs and Standards

- Import Tariffs
- Trade Barriers
- Import Requirements and Documentation
- U.S. Export Controls
- Temporary Entry
- Labeling and Marking Requirements
- Prohibited and Restricted Imports
- Customs Regulations and Contact Information
- Standards
- Trade Agreements
- Web Resources

Import Tariffs   Return to top

Singapore is generally a free port and an open economy. More than 99% of all imports into Singapore enter the country duty-free. For social and/or environmental reasons, Singapore levies high excise taxes on beer, wine and liquor, tobacco products, motor vehicles and petroleum products.

Singapore levies a 7% Goods and Services Tax (GST). For dutiable goods, the taxable value for GST is calculated based on the CIF (Cost, Insurance and Freight) value plus all duties and other charges. In the case of non-dutiable goods, GST will be based on the CIF value plus any commission and other incidental charges whether or not shown on the invoice. If the goods are dutiable, the GST will be collected simultaneously with the duties. Special provisions pertain to goods stored in licensed warehouses and free trade zones. See http://www.iras.gov.sg and http://www.customs.gov.sg

Inland Revenue Authority of Singapore
Comptroller of Goods & Service Tax
55 Newton Road
Revenue House
Singapore 307987
Tel: (65) 65/1800-356 8633 (General Helpline)
Fax: (65) 6351-3553
Email: gst@iras.gov.sg
Website: http://www.iras.gov.sg

Singapore Customs
55 Newton Road
#10-01 Revenue House
Singapore 307987
Tel: (65) 6355-2000 / 6355 2028
Fax: (65) 6250-8663

Email: customs_documentation@customs.gov.sg
Website: http://www.customs.gov.sg
Contact: Mdm. Fauziah Sani, Deputy Head, (Company Compliance Branch)
Email: Fauziah_Sani@customs.gov.sg

Trade Barriers   Return to top

Singapore maintains one of the most liberal trading regimes in the world, but U.S. companies face several trade barriers. Singapore maintains a tiered motorcycle operator licensing system based on engine displacement which, along with a road tax based on engine size, adversely affects U.S. exports of large motorcycles. Singapore also restricts the import and sale of non-medicinal chewing gum. For social and/or environmental reasons, it levies high excise taxes on distilled spirits and wine, tobacco products, and motor vehicles.

Services barriers include sectors such as pay TV, audiovisual and media services, legal services, banking, and cloud computing services for financial institutions. Details can be found in the USTR Report on Foreign Trade Barriers that is available on-line at http://www.ustr.gov/sites/default/files/2013%20NTE%20Singapore%20Final.pdf and http://www.ustr.gov/

Singapore's Agri-Food and Veterinary Authority (AVA) tests every imported shipment of meat and poultry and does not accept raw and uncooked poultry and meat products that contain salmonella bacteria that exceed AVA's unrealistic microbiological standards. This is not scientifically justifiable and has posed some difficulties for U.S. exporters.

After the discovery of BSE in the United States in December 2003, Singapore banned imports of all U.S. beef products, offals and variety meats. In January 2006, Singapore re-opened its markets to only U.S. boneless beef from animals under 30 months of age. Current World Organization for Animal Health (OIE) guidelines for BSE allow for the full range of beef and beef products from animals of any age and from countries categorized as controlled risk status for BSE. The United States was officially categorized by the OIE as negligible risk for BSE in May 2013. The United States continues to press Singapore to make science-based decisions based on OIE guidelines, which allow for the full-range of beef and beef products from animals of any age.

Import Requirements and Documentation   Return to top

Companies must make an inward declaration for all goods imported into Singapore. All imports require an import permit although this is largely a statistical requirement for most goods. Details can be found at
http://www.customs.gov.sg/leftNav/trad/Permits+and+Documentation.htm

Bona Fide Trade Samples

Import of trade samples that is below $330 (S$400) is not subject to payment of duty and/or GST. In addition, no permit is required for their import. Bona fide trade samples (excluding liquors and tobacco) may be imported if they are imported solely for the purpose of soliciting orders for goods to be supplied from abroad, for demonstration in

Singapore to enable manufacturers in Singapore to produce such articles to fulfill orders from abroad or by a manufacturer for the purpose of copying, testing or experimenting before they produce such articles in Singapore. More information can be found at http://www.customs.gov.sg/leftNav/trad/imp/Importation+of+Trade+Samples.htm

Medical and Medicinal Products Import Regulations

All medical devices and medicinal products, prescription and over-the-counter pharmaceuticals imported or sold in Singapore are required to be licensed by the Health Sciences Authority. The onus of applying for a product license rests with the license holder, i.e., a locally registered company that is responsible for the safety, quality and efficacy of the product. If U.S. companies have concerns regarding product licensing, they should contact the Health Sciences Authority (http://www.hsa.gov.sg) or ask a potential distributor to submit samples to the Health Sciences Authority.

U.S. Export Controls   Return to top

Companies wanting to export controlled items to Singapore must apply for licenses from the appropriate government agencies in the United States. U.S. goods being re-exported from intermediary consignees in Singapore to ultimate consignees in third countries require specific licensing. Singapore is a major transshipment hub for the Asian market. While many items may not initially require an export license, exporters need to be aware that two-thirds of items exported to Singapore are re-exported to third countries that may have more stringent licensing requirements that require additional export licenses.

The Bureau of Industry and Security (BIS) is responsible for implementing and enforcing the Export Administration Regulations (EAR), which regulate the export and re-export of certain commercial items while other U.S government agencies regulate more specialized exports. For example, the U.S. Department of State has authority over defense articles and defense services. A list of agencies involved in export controls can be found at www.bis.doc.gov or in Supplement No. 3 Part 730 of the EAR which is available on the Government Printing Office Website, www.gpo.gov. If you have any questions or would like information on export controls, please contact our Regional Export Control officer at http://export.gov/singapore/contactus/index.asp

Temporary Entry   Return to top

Goods may be temporarily imported under the Temporary Import Scheme for the purpose of repairs, displays, exhibitions or other similar events without the payment of duty and/or GST. A banker's guarantee is required under the Temporary Import Scheme. The temporary imports are covered by a Customs Inward Permit or a Carnet. Goods temporarily imported must be re-exported within the prescribed period using a Customs Outward permit. GST has to be paid if the goods are not subsequently re-exported. The procedures governing such importation can be found at http://www.customs.gov.sg/leftNav/trad/Temporary+Import+Scheme.htm

Admission Temporaire/Temporary Admission (ATA) Carnet

A foreign exhibitor may import exhibition goods into Singapore using an ATA carnet. When the exhibitor arrives in Singapore, the carnet must be produced together with the goods to Customs at the entry point for verification and endorsement. When goods covered by a carnet are taken out of Singapore, the foreign exhibitor must produce the carnet together with the goods to Customs at the exit point for verification and endorsement. GST will be recovered from the carnet holder on any item that is unaccounted for. For more information on Temporary Importation for Exhibition, Auction & Fairs or Temporary Import Scheme, please contact the following or visit http://www.customs.gov.sg/leftNav/trad/imp/Temporary+Importation+for+Exhibitions+Auctions+and+Fairs.htm

Singapore Customs
55 Newton Road
#10-01 Revenue House
Singapore 307987
Tel: (65) 6355-2000
Fax: (65) 6250-8663
Email: customs_documentation@customs.gov.sg
Website: http://www.customs.gov.sg

(Note: Chinese family names often precede given names; they are indicated in upper case letters)

Labeling and Marking Requirements   Return to top

Labels are required on imported food, drugs, liquors, paints and solvents and must specify the country of origin.

A food label should contain core information such as the prescribed food name, list of ingredients, mandatory warning, advisory statements or allergens declarations, net weight or volume, date mark, nutritional information panel, instructions for use or storage, country of origin, the name and address of the business and manufacturer and importer. Repackaged foods must be labeled to show (in English) the appropriate designation of food content printed in capital letters at least 1/16 inch high; whether foods are compounded, mixed or blended; the minimum quantity stated in metric net weight or measure; the name and address of the manufacturer or seller; and the country of origin. Illustrations must accurately describe the true nature or origin of the food. Foods having defined standards must be labeled to conform to those standards and be free from added foreign substances. Packages of food described as "enriched", "fortified", "vitaminized" or in any other way that implies that the article contains added vitamins or minerals must show the quantity of vitamins or minerals added per metric unit.

There are two levels of labeling requirements for medicinal products. Administrative labeling requirements are not statutory requirements and are specified in the Health Sciences Authority's Guidance on Medicinal Product Registration in Singapore. Compliance is checked during the product registration process, prior to granting of marketing approval. For legal labeling requirements, these are stipulated in the legislation related to medicinal products regulation in Singapore and are subject to the Health Sciences Authority's surveillance program. The labeling requirements include the name of the active ingredient, quantitative particulars, product license number and name

and address of the dealer. More information may be obtained at
http://www.hsa.gov.sg/publish/content/hsaportal/en/health_products_regulation.html

Labeling and advertising legislation also applies to the sale of vitamins and dietary supplements. Generally, labeling laws require that: 1) the composition of the products is disclosed in English, 2) labels/packaging materials not contain any references to diseases/conditions as specified in the schedule to the Medicines (Advertisement & Sale) Act (http://statutes.agc.gov.sg/aol/home.w3p); and 3) the advertising/sale promotion of the product in the public media be approved by the Health Sciences Authority.

Prohibited and Restricted Imports   Return to top

Special import licenses are required for certain goods, including strategic items, hazardous chemicals, radioactive materials, films and videos, arms and ammunition, agricultural biotechnology products, food derived from agricultural biotechnology products, medical devices, prescription drugs, over-the-counter drugs, vitamins with very high dosages of certain nutrients, and cosmetics and skin care products. The import of items such as lighters in the shape of pistols or revolvers, firecrackers, handcuffs, shell casings, and silencers is prohibited.

Generally, the import of goods that the government determines as posing a threat to health, security, safety and social decency is controlled. A full list of prohibited products and controlled goods and their corresponding controlling agencies can be obtained from the Singapore Customs website,
http://www.customs.gov.sg/leftnav/trad/tradenet/list+of+controlled+goods+-+imports.htm
http://www.customs.gov.sg/leftnav/trav/controlled+and+prohibited+goods.htm

Companies must make an outward declaration to export or re-export goods out of Singapore. Selected items are subjected to controls on exports of goods from Singapore. Items such as rubber, timber, granite, satellite dishes and receivers, and chlorofluorocarbons are subjected to export control and licensing. Items under export control must be endorsed or licensed by the appropriate government agencies before they can be exported. More information may be obtained at
http://www.customs.gov.sg/leftNav/trad/imp/Goods+Subject+to+Control.htm

The Strategic Trade Scheme (STS) is an enhanced permit regime that seeks to promote effective internal export control compliance and provide legitimate traders with greater facilitation in permit declarations involving transactions of strategic goods for non-WMD related end-use. The STS comprises 3 tiers whereby the level of facilitation and flexibility accorded to a company will be contingent upon their quality of internal export control compliance program. More information may be obtained at
http://www.customs.gov.sg/stgc/leftNav/per/Strategic+Trade+Scheme+%28STS%29.htm

Customs Regulations and Contact Information   Return to top

Customs Regulations

In Singapore, valuation for customs purposes is based on the Customs Valuation Code (CVC). The primary basis for Customs value is the transaction value of the imported goods when sold for export to Singapore. Where goods are dutiable, ad valorem or specific rates may be applied. An ad valorem rate, which is most commonly applied, is a percentage of the Customs value of the imported goods. A specific rate is a specified amount per unit of weight of other quantity.

Cost, insurance, freight, handling charges and all other charges incidental to the sale and delivery of the goods are taken into account when the duty is assessed. Exporters are required to ensure that the declared values of goods have not been undervalued or the Customs and Excise Department will increase the values declared. Severe penalties may be imposed on traders attempting to evade duty.

Free Trade Zone/Warehouses

Singapore has three Free Trade Zones (FTZ) authorities namely PSA Corporation Ltd, Jurong Port Pte Ltd and the Changi Airport Group (Singapore) Pte Ltd. The eight FTZs are Brani Terminal, Keppel Distripark, Pasir Panjang Terminal, Sembawang Wharves, Tanjong Pagar Terminal, Keppel Terminal, Jurong Port, Airport Logistics Park of Singapore and the Changi Airport Cargo Terminal Complex. They provide a wide range of facilities and services for storage and re-export of dutiable and controlled goods. Goods can be stored within the zones without any customs documentation until they are released in the market and they can also be processed and re-exported with minimum customs formalities. More information can be found at
http://www.customs.gov.sg/leftNav/trad/per/Documentation+in+a+Free+Trade+Zone.htm

GST is suspended for imported goods deposited in a FTZ and will only be payable upon removal from the FTZ for local consumption. GST is not payable on supply made in FTZ if the goods supplied are meant for transshipment or re-export.

The FTZs at the port facilitate entrepot trade and promote the handling of transshipment cargo. They offer free 72-hour storage for import/export of conventional and containerized cargo and 140-day free storage for transshipment/re-export cargo.

There are many warehouse space options available in Singapore. Some of the more popular ones are located close to the port and within easy reach of the airport and the Jurong industrial hub. These include the Tanjong Pagar, Alexandra and Pasir Panjang distriparks which are home to many established multinationals. The distriparks, in varying designs and size, cater to Central Distribution Center operators, manufacturers, traders, freight forwarders and others.
http://www.customs.gov.sg/leftNav/trad/dir/Licensed+Premises+for+Zero+GST+Goods.htm

Standards Return to top

- Overview
- Standards Organizations
- Conformity Assessment
- Product Certification
- Accreditation
- Publication of Technical Regulations
- Labeling and Marking

- Contacts

Overview Return to top

As the national standards and accreditation body, SPRING Singapore works in partnership with enterprises to develop a robust and internationally-recognized quality and standards infrastructure in Singapore. This quality and standards infrastructure enables enterprises to become more efficient, productive, global and competitive, as well as support national initiatives in health, safety, and protection of the environment. SPRING also encourages local industries and enterprises to adopt standards and conformance schemes to build trusted products and services.

To facilitate trade with Singapore's trading partners, SPRING has signed bilateral and multilateral Memorandum of Understanding (MOU) and Mutual Recognition Arrangements (MRA) with a number of agencies or governments around the world.

SPRING currently participates in a number of international or regional fora such as the Pacific Area Standards Congress (PASC), Asia Pacific Economic Cooperation (APEC) Sub-Committee on Standards & Conformance (SCSC), ASEAN Consultative Committee for Standards & Quality (ACCSQ), and Pacific Accreditation Cooperation (PAC).

SPRING also administers the SPRING's Business Excellence (BE) Initiative which helps organizations strengthen their management systems and processes for high performance. By adopting the internationally-benchmarked BE framework, organizations achieve key certification milestones and can also vie for the prestigious BE awards. The BE framework is aligned with excellence frameworks adopted for the US Malcolm Baldrige National Quality Award, EFQM (European Foundation for Quality Management) Excellence Award, Japan Quality Award and the Australian Business Excellence Awards. More information on the Business Excellence Initiative can be found at http://www.spring.gov.sg/qualitystandards/be/pages/business-excellence-initiative.aspx

Standards Organizations Return to top

The Singapore Standardisation Program is set up by SPRING to develop and promote Singapore Standards and International Standards which are important to Singapore. It establishes and publishes Singapore Standards by publication in the Government Gazette. SPRING is a member body of the International Organization for Standardization (ISO) and also a member body of the International Electrotechnical Commission (IEC) through the Singapore National Committee of the IEC.

SPRING facilitates the participation of industry in standards development work through the industry-led Singapore Standards Council. To strengthen its linkages with industry, the Council comprises standards partners or experts from the private and public sectors. The Standards Council approves the publication and withdrawal of Singapore Standards and Technical References and also oversees Singapore's participation in the development or monitoring of ISO and IEC international standards that are relevant to Singapore. It currently has 12 Standards Committees (SCs) to lead the development and promotion of standards in various industries or technical fields such as biomedical, building & construction, chemical, electrical & electronic, food and management systems. Under the various Standards Committees (SCs), Technical Committees (TCs) and Working Groups (WGs) are established to undertake the preparation and promotion of standards. Where possible, SPRING promotes the use of international standards. Singapore Standards are developed when there is no suitable international standards.

NIST Notify U.S. Service
Member countries of the World Trade Organization (WTO) are required under the Agreement on Technical Barriers to Trade (TBT Agreement) to report to the WTO all proposed technical regulations that could affect trade with other Member countries. **Notify U.S.** is a free, web-based e-mail subscription service that offers an opportunity to review and comment on proposed foreign technical regulations that can affect your access to international markets. Register online at Internet URL:
http://www.nist.gov/notifyus/

Conformity Assessment

A list of conformity assessment bodies accredited by the Singapore Accreditation Council (SAC) may be found here:
http://www.sac-accreditation.gov.sg/cab/acab/Pages/search_acab.aspx

Product Certification

A list of the designated product certification bodies for the Consumer Protection (Safety Requirements) Registration Scheme (CPS Scheme) administered by SPRING can be found here:
http://www.spring.gov.sg/QualityStandards/CPS/Documents/CPS_InfoBooklet.pdf

Accreditation

Besides being the national standards body in Singapore, SPRING also manages the Singapore Accreditation Council (SAC), the national accreditation body.

The SAC's primary function is to accredit Conformity Assessment Bodies (CAB) based on international standards. After being assessed on their competence, impartiality and performance capability to offer specified conformity assessment services, CABs gain the right of use of the SAC accreditation marks in their issuance of endorsed test/calibration/inspection reports or accredited certificates.

The Singapore Accreditation Council currently operates accreditation programs in the following areas:
- Calibration laboratories covering the temperature, dimensional, electrical and mechanical; and testing laboratories covering chemical, biological, environmental, medical, medical imaging, electrical, non-destructive testing, gaming and testing related to civil and mechanical engineering

- Inspection bodies for areas such as industrial pressure vessels and lifting equipment, motor vehicle, structural steelwork, cargo, technical audit for extension of pressure vessel, site investigation and hook lift & container .
- Quality management system (ISO 9001) certification bodies
- Environmental management system (ISO 14001) certification bodies.
- Product certification bodies
- Personnel certification bodies
- Occupational safety and health management system (OSHMS) certification bodies
- Hazard Analysis and Critical Control Points (HACCP) food safety management system certification bodies
- Food safety (ISO 22000) certification bodies
- Good Distribution Practice for Medical Device (GDPMDS) certification bodies
- Business continuity management certification bodies
- Energy management system (EnMS) certification bodies
- Proficiency Testing Providers

In October 2010, the SAC was formally recognised by the U.S. Environmental Protection Agency (EPA) for the ENERGY STAR Program. More information is available on the website: http://www.sac-accreditation.gov.sg.

The Singapore Accreditation Council has signed a number of accreditation related multilateral mutual recognition arrangements (MRAs/MLAs). These include:

- Asia Pacific Laboratory Accreditation Cooperation (APLAC) MRA for testing, calibration, medical (ISO 15189) and inspection
- Pacific Accreditation Cooperation (PAC) MLA for quality management system certification and product certification
- International Accreditation Forum (IAF) MLA for quality management system certification and product certification
- International Laboratory Accreditation Cooperation (ILAC) MRA for testing, calibration and inspection.

In addition, SPRING has appointed SAC as the Good Laboratory Practice (GLP) Compliance Monitoring Authority in Singapore. In January 2010, Singapore became a Mutual Acceptance of Data (MAD) adherent member of the Organization for Economic Cooperation and Development (OECD). This means that GLP studies conducted in Singapore for the health and safety assessment of chemicals will be accepted in more than 30 OECD and non-OECD member countries.

Singapore became the first country in Asia, and the third in the world (after the European Union and Canada), to operate a Mutual Recognition Arrangement (MRA) on telecom equipment certification with the U.S. The MRA provides for direct entry of telecommunications into either market without the need for additional testing and certification. Under the Asian Pacific Economic Cooperation (APEC) Telecommunications MRA implemented between the U.S. and Singapore, products can be tested and certified in the United States for conformance with Singapore's technical requirements. A list of the recognized U.S. testing and certification agencies can be found at: http://www.ida.gov.sg/Policies-and-Regulations/International-Relations-For-Telecom/Testing-Laboratories-and-Certification-Bodies-Recognised-by-IDA.

Publication of Technical Regulations   Return to top

Singapore Standards (SS) are nationally recognized documents that undergo the full consensus process, including a two-month public review before publication. They are functional or technical requirements in the form of specifications for materials, product system or process, codes of practice, methods of test, terminologies, and guides etc. It is voluntary in nature, except when referred to by the regulatory bodies in legislations. International standards can be adopted wholly or partially as Singapore Standards.

On the other hand, Technical Reference (TR) is transitional document developed to provide guidance for products and services where the users need to develop the TR quickly. It is a pre-standard for trial over a period of two years to assess on their suitability for the local industry. TRs can, therefore, become Singapore Standards after two years, continue as Technical References for further comments, or be withdrawn.

Both SSs and TRs are available for purchase in the Singapore Standards eShop. SPRING has appointed Toppan Leefung Pte Ltd to manage the sale of the Singapore Standards and Technical References, as well as international and overseas standards that SPRING is permitted to sell in Singapore. Toppan Leefung's contact details are:

Toppan Leefung Pte Ltd
1 Kim Seng Promenade #18-01
Great World City East Tower
Singapore 237994
Operating Hours:
Mon to Fri: 9.30am to 6.00pm
Closed on Saturdays, Sundays and Public Holidays
Customer Service Hotline: + (65) 6826 9691
Fax: + (65) 6820 3341
Email: singaporestandardseshop@toppanleefung.com
Singapore Standards eShop: http://www.singaporestandardseshop.sg

Labeling and Marking   Return to top

Regulation of consumer products

As the national safety authority and legal metrology authority for Singapore, SPRING administers two trust-marks, namely the SAFETY Mark and the Accuracy Label.

The "SAFETY Mark" is intended for selected electrical and electronics products as well as gas appliances which are sold to consumers in Singapore. The "SAFETY Mark" helps consumers and traders to identify registered controlled goods. All registered controlled goods must be tested to specific international and national safety standards and certified by designated product certification bodies. The products are individually marked with the "SAFETY Mark" either on the product or the packaging. The "SAFETY Mark" comprises a "safety logo" enclosed in a square on the left and the words "SAFETY MARK" within a rectangle on the right, and a set of 8-digit registration number that is unique and traceable to the registrant and the registered models. More information on the registration for the Safety Mark can be obtained from the website: http://www.spring.gov.sg/productsafety.

The "Accuracy Label" covers weighing and measuring instruments for trade use. In Singapore, all weighing and measuring instruments for trade use (like price computing scales in supermarkets, baggage weighing machines at airports and seaports as well as fuel dispensers at petrol stations) are regulated under the Singapore Weights and Measures Programme. Before an Accuracy Label could be affixed on these instruments, it would first need to be pattern registered with SPRING. Thereafter, every individual weighing or measuring instrument would need to be verified fit for trade use and affixed with a tamper-proof seal and the Accuracy Label by SPRING-appointed Authorised Verifiers (AVs).

Competent private sector bodies such as manufacturers, installers, suppliers and repairers of weighing and measuring instruments may apply to be designated by SPRING to handle the verification of weighing and measuring instruments for trade use. More information on the Accuracy Label can be obtained from the website: http://www.spring.gov.sg/wmo.

Telecommunication equipment imported for use in Singapore is subject to "Type Approval" by the Infocomm Development Authority of Singapore. More information can be obtained from the website: http://www.ida.gov.sg.

For the construction industry, the Building and Construction Authority uses the Construction Quality Assessment System (CONQUAS) to objectively rate building works. Details are available at the website: http://www.bca.gov.sg

Contacts Return to top

SPRING Singapore
1 Fusionopolis Walk
#01-02 South Tower, Solaris
Singapore 138628
Tel: (65) 6278 6666
Fax: (65) 6659 0640
Website: http://www.spring.gov.sg

Ms. CHANG Kwei Fern, Director, Accreditation Division
Email: sac@spring.gov.sg

Mr. CHEONG Tak Leong, Director, Standards Division
Email: standards@spring.gov.sg

Ms. LIM LeeFang, Deputy Director, Consumer Product Safety, Weights and Measures Office
Email: safety@spring.gov.sg

Ms TONG Shuh Lan, Director, Business Service Excellence Division
Email: be@spring.gov.sg

Standards contact at Commercial Service, Singapore:

Ms. CHIA Swee Hoon, Senior Commercial Specialist
Email: Sweehoon.chia@trade.gov

Trade Agreements   Return to top

As a nation with a small domestic market that depends on imports for food, energy and industrial raw materials, Singapore places the highest priority on the multilateral trading system embodied by the World Trade Organization (WTO). As a member of the WTO, Singapore believes that the WTO can provide a stable framework for developing sound multilateral rules that ensure that goods and services can flow freely with minimum impediment. The primary objective of Singapore's trade policy is to guard its trading interest by ensuring a free and open international trading environment.

In tandem with its support of the WTO, Singapore advocates that trade efforts are undertaken in the regional context such as APEC (Asia Pacific Economic Cooperation), ASEM (Asia-Europe Meeting) and ASEAN (Association of Southeast Asian Nations) as well as bilateral Free Trade Agreements (FTAs) to accelerate the momentum of trade liberalization and strengthen the multilateral trading system. It has actively pursued a number of legally binding arrangements with trading partners. ASEAN is preparing a roadmap for an ASEAN Economic Community by 2020 that aims to create a single enlarged market of 550 million people.

Singapore has concluded FTAs with the United States, ASEAN, Australia, New Zealand, Hashemite Kingdom of Jordan, China, India, Japan, South Korea, Costa Rica, Switzerland, Liechtenstein, Norway & Iceland, Gulf Cooperation Council, Panama, Peru and with Brunei, Chile and New Zealand under the Trans-Pacific SEP (Strategic Economic Partnership) Agreement. FTA negotiations are ongoing with Canada, Mexico, Pakistan and the Ukraine.

The Trans-Pacific Partnership (TPP) is an evolution of the Trans-Pacific Strategic Economic Partnership (TPSEP) between Singapore, Brunei, Chile and New Zealand. This was the result of the United States' interest in negotiating an FTA with the TPSEP member countries and subsequently joined by other countries like Australia, Peru, Vietnam and Malaysia. Formal negotiations commenced in March 2010 and are ongoing.

For more information, please visit http://www.iesingapore.gov.sg or http://www.fta.gov.sg

Web Resources   Return to top

Accounting and Corporate Regulatory Authority (ACRA)
http://www.acra.gov.sg

Agri-Food & Veterinary Authority of Singapore (AVA)
http://www.ava.gov.sg

Agency for Science, Technology & Research (A*STAR)
http://www.a-star.edu.sg

Building & Construction Authority of Singapore
http://www.bca.gov.sg

Civil Aviation Authority of Singapore (CAAS)
http://www.caas.gov.sg

Consumer Association of Singapore (CASE)
http://www.case.org.sg

Economic Development Board Singapore (EDB Singapore)
http://www.edb.gov.sg

Energy Market Authority (EMA)
http://www.ema.gov.sg

Enterprise One
http://www.enterpriseone.gov.sg/

Hotel Licensing Board (HLB)
http://www.hlb.gov.sg

Health Sciences Authority
http://www.hsa.gov.sg

Infocomm Development Authority of Singapore (IDA Singapore)
http://www.ida.gov.sg

International Enterprise Singapore (IE Singapore)
http://www.iesingapore.gov.sg

Intellectual Property Office of Singapore (IPOS)
http://www.ipos.gov.sg

International Revenue Authority of Singapore (IRAS)
http://www.iras.gov.sg

Information Technology Standards Committee
http://www.itsc.org.sg

Monetary Authority of Singapore (MAS)
http://www.mas.gov.sg

National Environment Agency (NEA)
http://www.nea.gov.sg

Ministry of Defence
http://www.mindef.gov.sg

Ministry of Education
http://www.moe.gov.sg

Ministry of Environment & Water Resources
http://www.mewr.gov.sg

Ministry of Finance
http://www.mof.gov.sg

Ministry of Health
http://www.moh.gov.sg

Ministry of Trade & Industry
http://www.mti.gov.sg

Singapore Customs
http://www.customs.gov.sg

NIST
www.nist.gov

Singapore Accreditation Centre
http://www.sac-accreditation.gov.sg

List of the recognized U.S. testing and certification agencies
http://www.ida.gov.sg/~/media/Files/PCDG/International%20Relations/ListRecoTestingLabsCertiBodies/RTL_USA.pdf

Consumer Protection (Safety Requirements) Registration Scheme
http://www.spring.gov.sg/QualityStandards/CPS/Documents/CPS_InfoBooklet.pdf

Singapore Standards eShop
http://www.singaporestandardseshop.sg

Spring Singapore (Singapore Productivity and Innovation for Growth)
http://www.spring.gov.sg

Infocomm Development Authority of Singapore
http://www.ida.gov.sg

Building and Construction Authority
http://www.bca.gov.sg

ASEAN Free Trade Area
http://www.aseansec.org

Return to table of contents

Return to table of contents

Chapter 6: Investment Climate

- Openness to Foreign Investment
- Conversion and Transfer Policies
- Expropriation and Compensation
- Dispute Settlement
- Performance Requirements and Incentives
- Right to Private Ownership and Establishment
- Protection of Property Rights
- Transparency of Regulatory System
- Efficient Capital Markets and Portfolio Investment
- Competition from State Owned Enterprises
- Corporate Social Responsibility
- Political Violence
- Corruption
- Bilateral Investment Agreements
- OPIC and Other Investment Insurance Programs
- Labor
- Foreign-Trade Zones/Free Ports
- Foreign Direct Investment Statistics
- Web Resources

Foreign investments, combined with investments through government-linked corporations (GLCs), underpin Singapore's open, heavily trade-dependent economy. With the exception of restrictions in the financial services, professional services, and media sectors, Singapore maintains a predominantly open investment regime. The World Bank's "Doing Business 2014" report ranked Singapore as the easiest country in which to do business. "The Global Competitiveness Report 2013-2014" by the World Economic Forum ranked Singapore as the second-most competitive economy globally. The U.S.-Singapore Free Trade Agreement (FTA), which came into force January 1, 2004, expanded U.S. market access in goods, services, investment, and government procurement, enhanced intellectual property protection, and provided for cooperation in promoting labor rights and the environment.

The Government of Singapore (GOS) is strongly committed to maintaining a free market but also takes a leadership role in planning Singapore's economic development. The government actively uses the public sector as both an investor and catalyst for development. As of end February 2014, the top six Singapore-listed GLCs accounted for about 17.3 percent of total capitalization of the Singapore Exchange (SGX). Some observers have criticized the dominant role of GLCs in the domestic economy, arguing that it has displaced or suppressed private sector entrepreneurship and investment.

Singapore's aggressive pursuit of foreign investment as another pillar of its overall economic strategy has enabled the country to evolve into a base for multinational corporations (MNCs). The Economic Development Board (EDB), Singapore's investment promotion agency, focuses on securing major investments in high value-added manufacturing and service activities as part of a strategy to replace labor-intensive, low value-added activities that have migrated offshore.

As part of the government's strategy to develop Singapore into a premier financial center, GOS offers tax incentives for financial institutions looking to set up operations. Further information, details and guidelines are available at http://www.mas.gov.sg/Singapore-Financial-Centre/Value-Propositions/Setting-Up.aspx.

Relevant Rankings and Figures

Measure	Year	Ranking
TI Corruption Index	2013	#5
Heritage Economic Freedom	2013	#2
World Bank Doing Business	2014	#1

Openness to Foreign Investment   Return to top

Singapore's legal framework and public policies are generally favorable toward foreign investors. Foreign investors are not required to enter into joint ventures or cede management control to local interests, and local and foreign investors are subject to the same basic laws. Apart from regulatory requirements in some sectors (see "Limits on National Treatment and Other Restrictions"), the government screens investment proposals only to determine eligibility for various incentive regimes (see Annex). Singapore places no restrictions on reinvestment or repatriation of earnings or capital. The judicial system upholds the sanctity of contracts, and decisions are effectively enforced.

Limits on National Treatment and Other Restrictions: Exceptions to Singapore's general openness to foreign investment exist in telecommunications, broadcasting, the domestic news media, financial services, legal, and other professional services, and property ownership. Under Singapore law, Articles of Incorporation may include shareholding limits that restrict ownership in corporations by foreign persons.

Telecommunications: The Telecoms Competition Code opened the industry in 2000 to foreign or domestic companies seeking to provide facilities-based (fixed line or mobile) or services-based (local, international, and callback) telecommunications services. Singapore Telecommunications (SingTel), the former monopoly and currently 52-percent government-owned, faces competition in all market segments. Its main competitors, MobileOne and StarHub, are also GLCs. As of March 1 2014, Singapore has 53 facilities-based (group) and 258 services-based (individual) operators.

Since January 2007, SingTel has been exempted from dominant licensee obligations for the residential and commercial portions of the retail international telephone services. SingTel has already been exempted from dominant licensee obligations for wholesale international telephone services since November 2003. IDA decided in June 2009, following a formal public consultation held in late 2008, that SingTel will be exempted from dominant licensee obligations for two services, i.e., Terrestrial International Private Leased Circuit, and Backhaul. SingTel has already been exempted from dominant licensee obligations for International Managed Data Services since April 2005.

U.S. and other companies remain concerned about the lack of transparency in some aspects of Singapore's telecommunications regulatory and rule-making process. In particular, there is no obligation to make information publicly available concerning a company's request for a stay of decision or the filing of an appeal, request public comments about such requests, or to publish a detailed explanation concerning final decisions made by the Infocomm Development Authority (IDA) or the Ministry of Communication and Information (MCI).

Infrastructure for the next generation access network, a national broadband all-fiber network, is being built by OpenNet, a consortium formed by Canada's Axia Netmedia (which holds 30-percent ownership), SingTel (30 percent), Singapore Press Holdings (25 percent), and SP Telecommunications (15 percent). The network will be operated by Nucleus Connect, a wholly-owned subsidiary of StarHub. Operational separation is imposed on Nucleus Connect to maintain its independence from OpenNet, and to ensure that it provide services to all downstream operators on the same prices and terms and conditions, with the same processes and access to information. About 95 percent of homes and offices have been hooked up to the fiber-optic broadband network as of end October 2012. When fully completed, the broadband network may allow fuller access to telecom services providers to reach homes and businesses without requiring access to SingTel-owned circuits.

OpenNet has been saddled with delays in delivering fibre broadband services across Singapore. OpenNet was fined $81,653 (S$100,000) for delaying the supply of cooling services to internet service providers in October 2012. In November 2013, IDA fined OpenNet another $601,250 (S$ 750,000) for not meeting its obligation to the IDA to roll out the network to all homes and offices here by the end of 2012 and to penalize Opennet for not fulfilling its duty to connect 98 percent of residential sign-ups within three working days of receiving their orders.

In August 2013, NetLink Trust unveiled its plan to buy OpenNet from its existing shareholders for $98.92 million (S$ 126 million). SingTel is the initial and sole unit holder of NetLink Trust. NetLink Trust is a business trust that owns the ducts and manholes through which the optical fibre cables pass to reach homes and buildings. Under the agreement, NetLink Trust will have control over all the steps involved in connecting users to the network, from building the fibre and owning the manholes and ducts along which it travels, to deploying the manpower needed to roll it out to buildings and homes. As a result, consumers should expect improved operational efficiencies and one point of accountability.

In September 2013, seven Singapore telecommunication firms, including M1 and StarHub, voiced their opposition to SingTel's proposed acquisition of OpenNet. noting that the proposed consolidation would see SingTel becoming the 100 percent beneficial owner of the only other nationwide fixed telecommunications network in Singapore, apart from SingTel's own network. The companies said the unprecedented show of solidarity demonstrates the grave concerns the industry has over the competition issues raised by the proposed consolidation, including the potential of discriminatory treatment and a lack of independence. In November 2013, IDA's approved the deal, but it comes with several conditions so as to allay fears that the deal could potentially lead to anti-competitive practices. The conditions include IDA establishing a monitoring board consisting of government representatives to ensure SingTel does not influence any decisions on service price as well as terms and conditions. SingTel must also divest its majority stake in NetLink Trust by April 2018. The deal was officially completed by end November 2013, with SingTel accepting all conditions set by IDA.

In November 2011, the GOS amended the Telecommunications Act, giving it more power to curb monopolistic behavior in the telecommunications sector and ensure continuity in services. The aim is to ensure the sector remains competitive. The new law paves the way for the Government to issue a Separation Order to a telecommunications company (Telco) that engages in anti-competitive behavior. Such an order would require the Telco to divest of its assets or business to a separate entity, to ensure equal and open access. The GOS has assured businesses that it does not intend to exercise this power "frivolously", and it can do so only as a "last resort" if other measures are insufficient in enhancing competition. The amendment also empowers the Minister of Communication and Information to issue Special Administrative Orders (SAOs). An SAO is an order from the Minister directing the takeover of control of a telecommunication licensee's affairs, business and property by another party, so as to ensure that a key telecommunication network or service continues to be functional, for public and national interest. Another amendment revises the maximum administrative financial penalty on Telco that breach regulations to 10% of the annual business turnover for licensable services of a licensee, or US$ 790,514 (S$1 million), whichever is higher. This is to ensure that the penalty framework continues to act as a sufficient deterrent to secure licensees' compliance to regulatory conditions. If the penalty is not paid within a specified period, the IDA can cancel or suspend a part of or the whole license given to a Telco, or reduce the license period.

Media: The local free-to-air broadcasting, cable and newspaper sectors are effectively closed to foreign firms. Section 47 of the Broadcasting Act restricts foreign equity ownership of companies broadcasting to the Singapore domestic market to 49 percent or less, although the Act does allow for exceptions. Individuals cannot hold more than three percent of the ordinary shares issued by a broadcasting company without the government's prior approval.

The Newspaper and Printing Presses Act restricts equity ownership (local or foreign) to five percent per shareholder and requires that directors be Singapore citizens. Newspaper companies must issue two classes of shares, ordinary and management, with the latter available only to Singapore citizens or corporations approved by the government. Holders of management shares have an effective veto over selected board decisions. The government controls distribution, importation and sale of any "declared" foreign newspaper, and significantly restricts freedom of the press, having curtailed or banned the circulation of some foreign publications. The government has also "gazetted" foreign newspapers, i.e., numerically limited their circulation. Singapore's leaders have brought defamation suits against foreign publishers. Such suits have resulted in the foreign publishers issuing apologies and paying damages.

While local media is heavily government influenced, in practice there are few restrictions on the internet, and Singaporeans generally have uncensored access to international media. However, the Media Development Authority (MDA), which is responsible for regulating Internet service providers, has blocked various websites containing objectionable material, such as pornography and racist and religious hatred sites.

Licensing scheme for news websites: In May, 2013 the Media Development Authority announced a new regulation requiring certain internet news sites to obtain a license. This requirement applies to sites that publish on average over a two-month period one article per week relating to issues in Singapore and which receive a two-month average of at least 50,000 monthly site visits from unique addresses of Singapore-based internet providers. The license requires these sites to submit a bond of S$50,000 ($40,000) and to adhere to new requirements to remove prohibited content within 24 hours of notification from the MDA. Some citizens viewed this regulation as a way to censor online critics of the government. In June 2013 more than 2,500 persons participated in a protest against the new regulation. The MDA stated that it put the regulation in place to regulate commercial news sites and promote conformity with other forms of media such as print and television. The minister of communications and information publicly stated that the new regulation was not intended to target individual bloggers or blogs.

MediaCorp TV is the only free-to-air TV broadcaster; the government owns 80 percent and SGX listed Singapore Press Holdings (SPH) owns the remaining 20 percent. Pay-TV providers StarHub Cable Vision (SCV) and MioTV are wholly-owned subsidiaries of StarHub and SingTel, respectively. Free-to-air radio broadcasters are mainly government-owned, with MediaCorp Radio Singapore being the largest operator. BBC World Services is the only foreign free-to-air broadcaster in Singapore.

The Media Development Authority (MDA) introduced new cross-carriage measures in March 2010 that would require pay TV companies to cross carry content subject to exclusive carriage provisions. Henceforth, a pay TV company with an exclusive contract for a channel would be required to share that content with other pay TV companies at their request. Content providers consider the measures an unnecessary interference in a competitive market that would deny content holders the ability to negotiate freely in the marketplace, and an interference with their ability to manage and protect their intellectual property. The policy took effect August 1, 2011. According to MDA, the key objective of the cross-carriage measure was to rectify the high degree of content fragmentation in the Singapore pay-TV market, and shift the focus of competition from an exclusivity-centric strategy to other aspects such as service differentiation and competitive packaging. In practice, the provision is creating headaches, most recently leading the MDA to get involved in a messy contract dispute between SingTel and StarHub, Singapore's two leading pay-TV platforms, over the cross-carriage of the English Premier (soccer) League (EPL). MDA eventually ordered SingTel to make its EPL content available to StarHub customers, even though SingTel claimed to have signed a non-exclusive contract. The dispute has resulted in higher EPL pricing and unhappy consumers, leading to speculation that MDA will undertake a review of the cross-carriage mechanism. More common content is now available across the different pay-TV platforms, , and the operators are beginning to differentiate themselves by originating their own content, offering subscribed content online via PCs and tablet computers, and delivering content via fibre networks.

Banking: The Monetary Authority of Singapore (MAS) regulates all banking activities as provided for under the Banking Act. Singapore maintains legal distinctions between foreign and local banks, and the type of license (i.e., full service, wholesale, and offshore) held by foreign banks. As of March 11, 2014 28 foreign full service licensees,

55 wholesale licensees, and 37 offshore licensees operated in Singapore. All offshore banks are eligible to be upgraded to wholesale bank status based on MAS criteria to enable them to conduct a wider range of activities. Except in retail banking, Singapore laws do not distinguish operationally between foreign and domestic banks.

The government initiated a banking liberalization program in 1999 to ease restrictions on foreign banks and has supplemented this with phased-in provisions under the FTA. These measures include removal of a 40-percent ceiling on foreign ownership of local banks and a 20-percent aggregate foreign shareholding limit on finance companies. The Minister in charge of the Monetary Authority of Singapore must approve the merger or takeover of a local bank or financial holding company, as well as the acquisition of voting shares in such institutions above specific thresholds of 5 percent, 12 percent or 20 percent of shareholdings. Although GOS has lifted the formal ceilings on foreign ownership of local banks and finance companies, the approval of controllers of local banks ensures that this control rests with individuals or groups whose interests are aligned with the long term interests of the Singapore economy and Singapore's national interests. Of the 28 full service licenses granted to foreign banks, four have gone to U.S. banks. Ten of the 28 full service licensees (including one U.S. bank) have been granted "qualifying full bank" (QFB) status. U.S. financial institutions enjoy phased-in benefits under the FTA. Since January 2006, U.S.-licensed full service banks that are also QFBs have been able to operate at an unlimited number of locations (branches or off-premises ATMs) versus 25 for non-U.S. full service foreign banks with QFB status. U.S. and foreign full-service banks with QFB status can freely relocate existing branches and share ATMs among themselves. They can also provide electronic funds transfer and point-of-sale debit services, and accept services related to Singapore's compulsory pension fund.

Locally and non-locally incorporated subsidiaries of U.S. full-service banks with QFB status can apply for access to local ATM networks. However, no U.S. bank has come to a commercial agreement to gain such access. Singapore lifted its quota on new licenses for U.S. wholesale banks in January 2007. Singapore abolished quotas on new licenses for full-service foreign banks in July 2005.

Despite liberalization, U.S. and other foreign banks in the domestic retail banking sector still face barriers. However, under the enhanced QFB program launched in June 2012, a few banks with significant retail operations in Singapore may be granted an additional 25 places of business, of which up to 10 may be branches. But MAS will require that the bank be locally incorporated with a majority Singaporean or permanent resident board representation. Local incorporation will give retail depositors an extra safeguard. Local retail banks do not face similar constraints on customer service locations or access to the local ATM network. Holders of credit cards issued locally by foreign banks or other financial institutions sometimes cannot access their accounts through the local ATM networks. They are also unable to access their accounts for cash withdrawals, transfers or bill payments at ATMs operated by banks other than those operated by their own bank or at foreign banks' shared ATM network. Nevertheless, full-service foreign banks have made significant inroads in other retail banking areas, with substantial market share in products like credit cards and personal and housing loans.

U.S. industry advocates enhancements to Singapore's credit bureau system, in particular, adoption of an open admission system for all lenders, including non-banks.

There are currently two credit bureaus in Singapore, Credit Bureau (Singapore) Private Ltd. ("CBS") and Credit Scan.

Securities and Asset Management: Singapore has no trading restrictions on foreign-owned stockbrokers. There is no cap on the aggregate investment by foreigners regarding the paid-up capital of dealers that are members of the SGX. Direct registration of foreign mutual funds is allowed, provided MAS approves the prospectus and the fund. The FTA has relaxed conditions that foreign asset managers must meet in order to offer products under the government-managed compulsory pension fund (Central Provident Fund Investment Scheme).

Legal Services: As of end 2013, 12 of the 114 foreign law firms in Singapore were from the United States. In December 2008, Singapore granted Qualifying Foreign Law Practice (QFLP) licenses to six foreign law firms (including two U.S. firms) to practice Singapore law, although restrictions remain in certain areas, including conveyance, criminal law, family law, and domestic litigation. In 1Q 2013, Singapore awarded another four QFLP licenses during the second round of applications, which ended in 2012 and attracted twenty three applicants. Three of these firms were U.S. companies. In total, ten QFLP licences have been issued since 2008, with five of them issued to U.S. firms. They are Gibson, Dunn & Crutcher; Jones Day; Sidley Austin; White & Case; and Latham & Watkins. Foreign law firms can otherwise provide legal services in relation to Singapore law only through a Joint Law Venture (JLV) or Formal Law Alliance (FLA) with a Singapore law firm, in accordance with the relevant legislation. The Joint Law Venture is collaboration between a Foreign Law Practice and Singapore Law Practice. There is no express prescription regarding the shares in that collaboration that can be held by either of the constituent parties. It is expected the shareholdings in that collaboration would be agreed between the constituent parties as equals. The Attorney-General will consider all the relevant circumstances including the proposed structure and its overall suitability to achieve the objectives for which Joint law Ventures are permitted to be established in deciding on its approval. Currently, there are no U.S. Joint Law Ventures. U.S. and foreign attorneys are allowed to represent parties in arbitration without the need for a Singapore attorney to be present. With the exception of law degrees from a handful of designated U.S., British, Australian, and New Zealand universities, no foreign university law degrees are recognized for purposes of admission to practice law in Singapore. Under the FTA, Singapore recognizes law degrees from Harvard University, Columbia University, New York University, and the University of Michigan. Singapore will admit to the Bar Singapore-citizen or permanent-resident law school graduates of those designated universities who are ranked among the top 70 percent of their graduating class or have obtained lower-second class honors (under the British system).

Engineering and Architectural Services: Engineering and architectural firms can be 100 percent foreign-owned. Only engineers and architects registered with the Professional Engineers Board and the Architects Board, respectively, can practice in Singapore. All applicants (both local and foreign) must have at least four years of practical experience in engineering or architectural works, and pass an examination set by the respective Board.

Accounting and Tax Services: The major international accounting firms operate in Singapore. Public accountants and at least one partner of a public accounting firm must reside in Singapore. Only public accountants who are members of the Institute of Certified Public Accountants of Singapore and registered with the Public Accountants

Board may practice in Singapore. The Board recognizes U.S. accountants registered with the American Institute of Certified Public Accountants.

Real Estate: Foreigners are not allowed to purchase public housing (HDB) in Singapore. Under the Residential Property Act, foreigners are allowed to purchase private sector housing (condominiums or any unit within a building) without the need to obtain prior approval from the Singapore Land Authority. However, foreigners are not allowed to acquire all the apartments within a building or all the units in an approved condominium apartment without prior approval. For landed homes (houses) and vacant residential land, prior approval is required. There are no restrictions on foreign ownership of industrial and commercial real estate. In December 2011, the GOS enacted an additional effective 10% tax on foreigners who purchase homes in Singapore. In January 2013, GOS further raised the Additional Buyer's Stamp Duty to 15%, however, U.S. citizens are exempt from this tax due to the U.S.-Singapore FTA.

Energy: Singapore completed efforts to liberalize its gas market with the amendment of the Gas Act and implementation of a Gas Network Code in 2008, which were designed to give gas retailers and importers direct access to the onshore gas pipeline infrastructure. However, key parts of the local gas market, such as gas retailing and access to offshore gas pipelines, remain controlled by incumbent Singaporean firms. In the past, the dominance of Singaporean government-linked corporations in this sector proved challenging for American companies that tried to enter the power generation and gas import business.

Conversion and Transfer Policies   Return to top

The FTA commits Singapore to the free transfer of capital, unimpeded by regulatory restrictions. Singapore places no restrictions on reinvestment or repatriation of earnings and capital, and maintains no significant restrictions on remittances, foreign exchange transactions and capital movements. (See "Efficient Capital Markets" for a discussion of certain restrictions on the borrowing of Singapore Dollars (SGD) for use offshore.)

Expropriation and Compensation   Return to top

The FTA contains strong investor protection provisions relating to expropriation and due process; provisions are in place for fair market value compensation for any expropriated investment.

Singapore has not expropriated property owned by foreign investors and has no laws that force foreign investors to transfer ownership to local interests. No significant disputes are pending.

Singapore has signed investment promotion and protection agreements with a wide range of countries (see "Bilateral Investment Agreements" below). These agreements mutually protect nationals or companies of either country against war and non-commercial risks of expropriation and nationalization for an initial period of 15 years and continue thereafter unless otherwise terminated.

Dispute Settlement   Return to top

All core obligations of the FTA are subject to the dispute settlement provisions of the Agreement. The dispute settlement procedures promote compliance through consultation and trade-enhancing remedies, rather than relying solely on trade sanctions. The procedures also set higher standards of openness and transparency. Singapore enacted and subsequently amended the Arbitration Act of 2001 for domestic arbitration based on the United Nations Commission on International Trade Law (UNCITRAL) Model Law. Singapore ratified the recognition and enforcement of Foreign Arbitration Awards (New York, 1958) on August 21, 1986, and the International Convention on the Settlement of Investment Disputes on November 13, 1968. The Singapore International Arbitration Center (SIAC) and the Singapore Mediation Center (SMC) actively promote mediation and reconciliation for settling commercial disputes.

Performance Requirements and Incentives   Return to top

In general, Singapore complies with WTO Trade-Related Investment Measures (TRIMS) obligations. The FTA prohibits and removes certain performance-related restrictions on U.S. investors such as limitations on the number of customer service locations for the retail banking sector.

There are no discriminatory or preferential export or import policies affecting foreign investors. The government does not require investors to purchase from local sources or specify a percentage of output for export. The government also does not require local equity ownership in the investment. There are no rules forcing the transfer of technology. Foreign investors face no requirement to reduce equity over time and are free to obtain their necessary financing from any source. Employment of host country nationals is not required.

Singapore offers numerous incentives to encourage foreign investors to startup businesses; particularly in targeted growth sectors (see Annex).

Right to Private Ownership and Establishment   Return to top

Foreign and local entities may readily establish, operate, and dispose of their own enterprises in Singapore. Except for representative offices (where foreign firms maintain a local representative but do not conduct commercial transactions in Singapore), there are no restrictions on carrying out remunerative activities.

All businesses in Singapore must be registered with the Accounting and Corporate Regulatory Authority. Foreign investors can operate their businesses in one of the following forms: sole proprietorship, limited partnership, incorporated company, foreign company branch or representative office.

Private businesses, both local and foreign, compete on a generally equal basis with GLCs, although some observers have complained that GLCs benefit from cheaper financing due to an implicit government guarantee. Singapore officials reject such assertions, arguing that the government does not interfere with the operations of GLCs or grant them special privileges, preferential treatment or hidden subsidies, adding that GLCs are subject to the same regulatory regime and discipline of the market as private sector companies. Many observers, however, have been critical of cases where GLCs have entered into new lines of business or where government agencies have "corporatized" certain government functions, in both circumstances entering into competition with already-existing private businesses.

The FTA contains specific conduct guarantees to ensure that GLCs will operate on a commercial and non-discriminatory basis towards U.S. firms. GLCs with substantial revenues or assets are also subject to enhanced transparency requirements under the FTA. In accordance with its FTA commitments, Singapore enacted the Competition Act in 2004 and established the Competition Commission of Singapore in January 2005. The Act contains provisions on anti-competitive agreements, decisions, and practices; abuse of dominance; enforcement and appeals process; and mergers and acquisitions.

Singapore has an extensive network of GLCs that are active in many sectors of the economy. Some sectors, notably telecommunications and financial services, are subject to sector-specific regulatory bodies and competition regulations typically less rigorous than those being implemented under the Competition Act.

Protection of Property Rights   Return to top

In line with its FTA commitments and obligations under international treaties and conventions, Singapore has developed one of the stronger intellectual property rights (IPR) regimes in Asia, although concerns remain in certain areas such as business software piracy, online piracy and enforcement. Singapore has taken steps to bring its IPR laws in line with international standards, including amending its Trademarks Act, Patents Act, the Layout Designs of Integrated Circuits Act, Registered Designs Act, and new Plant Varieties Protection Act. In accordance with its FTA obligations, Singapore has implemented Article 1 through Article 6 of the Joint Recommendation concerning Provisions on the Protection of Well-Known Marks of 1999. It has signed and ratified the International Convention for the Protection of New Varieties of Plants (1991) and the Convention Relating to the Distribution of Program-Carrying Signals Transmitted by Satellite (1974).

Singapore is a member of the WTO and a party to the Agreement on Trade-Related Aspects of Intellectual Property Rights (TRIPS). It is a signatory to other international copyright agreements, including the Paris Convention, the Berne Convention, the Patent Cooperation Treaty, the Madrid Protocol, and the Budapest Treaty. The World Intellectual Property Organization (WIPO) Secretariat opened offices in Singapore in 2005 (http://www.wipo.int/about-wipo/en/offices/singapore/). Amendments to the Trademark Act, which took effect in January 2007, fulfill Singapore's obligations in WIPO's revised Treaty on the Law of Trademarks.

According to industry estimates, between 45 and 50 per cent of Internet users in Singapore accessed unlicensed sites which illegally host music and movies, among other files, for free downloading in early 2012. Facing reports stating Singapore has the highest incidence of per-capita infringement in Asia, the Ministry of Law is proposing changes to its laws that will allow rights owners, or the exclusive licensees of the work, to directly apply for a court injunction to block off public access to the pirated material.

The proposal was opened for public consultation through April, 2014. Notably, the proposed changes to the law are targeted at those who clearly and blatantly infringe copyright, rather than search engines or websites based primarily on user-generated content.Music and film industry representatives remain concerned that Internet piracy will continue to rise as Singapore expands access to its high-speed broadband network. The FTA ensures that government agencies will not grant approval to patent-violating products, but Singapore does allow parallel imports. Under the amended Patents Act, the patent owner has the right to bring an action to stop an importer of "grey market goods" from importing the patent owner's patented product if the product has not previously been sold or distributed in Singapore.

The FTA ensures protection of test data and trade secrets submitted to the government for product approval purposes. Disclosure of such information is prohibited for a period of five years for pharmaceuticals and ten years for agricultural chemicals. Singapore has no specific legislation concerning trade secrets. Instead, it protects investors' commercially valuable proprietary information under common law by the Law of Confidence. U.S. industry has expressed concern that this provision is inadequate.

Transparency of Regulatory System   Return to top

The FTA enhances transparency by requiring regulatory authorities, to the extent possible, to consult with interested parties before issuing regulations, to provide advance notice, and comment periods for proposed rules, and to publish all regulations.

The government has established a centralized Internet portal -- www.reach.gov.sg -- to solicit feedback on selected draft legislation and regulations, a process that is being used with increasing frequency. As noted in the "Openness to Foreign Investment" section, some U.S. companies, in particular, in the telecommunications and media sectors, are concerned about the government's lack of transparency in its regulatory and rule-making process.

Singapore strives to promote an efficient, business-friendly regulatory environment. Tax, labor, banking and finance, industrial health and safety, arbitration, wage and training rules and regulations are formulated and reviewed with the interests of both foreign investors and local enterprises in mind. Starting in 2005, a Rules Review Panel, comprising senior civil servants, began overseeing a review of all rules and regulations; this process will be repeated every five years. A Pro-Enterprise Panel of high-level public sector and private sector representatives examines feedback from businesses on regulatory issues and provides recommendations to the government.

Local laws give regulatory bodies wide discretion to modify regulations and impose new conditions, but in practice agencies use this positively to adapt incentives or other services on a case-by-case basis to meet the needs of foreign as well as domestic companies.

Procedures for obtaining licenses and permits are generally transparent and not burdensome, but some exceptions apply. Procedures can be faster for investors in areas considered national priorities. Singapore has established an online licensing portal to provide a one-stop application point for multiple licenses -- https://licences.business.gov.sg.

Corporate Governance: Singapore has a private sector-led Council on Corporate Disclosure and Governance to implement the country's Code of Corporate Governance. Compliance with the Code is not mandatory but listed companies are required under the Singapore Exchange Listing Rules to disclose their corporate governance practices and give explanations for deviations from the Code in their annual reports.

Accounting Standards: Singapore's prescribed accounting standards ("Financial Reporting Standards" or FRS) are aligned with those of the International Accounting Standards Board. Companies can deviate from these standards when required to present a "true and fair" set of financial statements. Singapore-incorporated, publicly-listed companies can use certain alternative standards such as International Accounting Standards (IAS) or the U.S. Generally Accepted Accounting Principles (U.S. GAAP) if they are listed on foreign stock exchanges that require these standards. They do not need to reconcile their accounts with FRS. All other Singapore-incorporated companies must use FRS unless the Accounting and Corporate Regulatory Authority exempts them.

Efficient Capital Markets and Portfolio Investment   Return to top

Singapore actively facilitates the free flow of financial resources. Credit is allocated on market terms and foreign investors can access credit, U.S. dollars, Singapore dollars (SGD), and other foreign currencies on the local market. The Monetary Authority of Singapore (MAS) formulates and implements the country's monetary and exchange rate policy, and supervises and regulates the country's sophisticated financial and capital markets.

Total assets under management in Singapore stood at $1.30 trillion at the end of 2012, a 21.5 percent year-on-year increment in view of strong inflows and higher market valuations. About 80 percent of the funds managed in Singapore are foreign sourced, with over 70 percent of these funds invested in the Asia-Pacific region. The government has sought to boost the country's asset management sector by placing with foreign-owned firms a significant portion of government reserves managed by the Government of Singapore Investment Corporation (GIC). Singapore-based companies issued approximately US$ 14.1 billion in bonds in the first 10 months of 2013, down sharply from US$31.2 billion in the same period in 2012.

Singapore's banking system is sound and well-regulated. Total domestic banking assets were about US$777.68 billion as of December 2013. Local Singapore banks are relatively small by regional standards, but are reasonably profitable and have stronger capital levels and credit ratings than many of their peers in the region. As of fourth quarter 2013, the non-performing loans (NPLs) ratio of the three local banks averaged 1.0 percent. Banks are statutorily prohibited from engaging in non-financial business. Banks can hold 10 percent or less in non-financial companies as an "equity portfolio investment."

The Securities and Futures Act (SFA) of 2002 moved Singapore's capital markets to a disclosure-based regime. The SFA allows for imposition of civil or criminal penalties against corporations listed on the Singapore Exchange (SGX) that fail to disclose material information on a continuous basis. Listed companies are required to prepare quarterly financial reporting. The SFA requires persons acquiring shareholdings of five percent or more of the voting shares of a listed company to disclose such acquisitions as well as any subsequent changes in their holdings directly to the SGX within two business days. The SFA also contains enhanced market misconduct provisions. The Act was further strengthened in 2009 to provide for stronger market misconduct enforcement with the courts empowered to order disgorgement of gains from illegal trades, and allowing the transfer of evidence between the Commercial Affairs Department of the police force and MAS.

Competition from State Owned Enterprises   Return to top

Singapore has an extensive network of government-linked corporations (GLC) that are fully or partially owned by Temasek Holdings, a holding company with the Singapore Ministry of Finance as its sole shareholder. As previously noted, Singapore GLCs are active in many sectors of the economy, especially strategically important sectors like telecommunications, media, public transportation, defense, port, and airport operations. In addition, the GLCs are also present in many other sectors of the economy, including banking, shipping, airline, consumer/lifestyle, infrastructure, and real estate.

GLCs operate on a commercial basis and have no specific advantage in competing with private enterprises based on their government ownership. However, some private sector companies have said they encountered unfair business practices and opaque bidding processes that appeared to favor incumbent, government-linked firms.

GLCs' corporate governance is guided by policies developed by Temasek Holdings. However, there are differences in corporate governance disclosures and practices across them and GLC boards are allowed to determine their own governance practices. GLC board seats are not specifically allocated to government officials, although retired officials are often represented on boards and fill senior management positions.

There are two sovereign wealth funds (SWF) in Singapore, the Government of Singapore Investment Corporation (GIC) and the previously- mentioned Temasek Holdings. The government established the two SWFs to manage Singapore's substantial investments, fiscal, and foreign reserves.

GIC, Singapore's largest SWF with an estimated $220 billion in assets, does not invest domestically. GIC manages Singapore's international investments, which are generally passive (non-controlling) investments in publicly-traded entities. Its investment is entirely overseas, with the United States as its top destination, accounting for 36 percent of GIC's portfolio as of March 2013. Although not required by law, since 2008 GIC has published an annual report describing its management and governance, and how it invests Singapore's foreign reserves.

Temasek began as a holding company for Singapore's state-owned enterprises, but has since branched to other asset classes and generally focuses on holding significant (often controlling) stakes in companies. As of March 2013, Temasek's exposure to Singapore was 30%, with the rest of Asia accounting for 41% of its portfolio. Temasek's stated goal is to hold and manage the government's investments in companies for the long-term benefit of Singapore, to create jobs, and contribute to Singapore's economic survival, progress and prosperity. Temasek formerly focused on managing industries to promote economic development, but has shifted emphasis to commercial objectives and principles. Temasek exercises its shareholder rights to influence the strategic directions of its companies but does not get involved in the day-to-day business and commercial decisions of its firms and subsidiaries. Temasek publishes an annual report, but only provides consolidated financial statements, which aggregate all of Temasek's subsidiaries into a single financial report.

Corporate Social Responsibility

The awareness and implementation of CSR in Singapore has been increasing since the government's formation of the Singapore Compact, a national society promoting CSR in Singapore. In May 2004, the National Tripartite Committee on CSR was established to study the issues holistically and address any gaps at the national level. The initiative provides strategic direction and overall coordination for various CSR programs, which include helping small and medium-sized enterprises (SMEs) adopt good CSR practices. In January 2005, the Singapore Compact for Corporate Social Responsibility was set up to provide a forum for collaboration, support, and information sharing on good CSR practices.

In October 2008, a National CSR Survey released by the Singapore Compact showed that 40% of the 507 Singapore-based companies surveyed were aware of CSR. The awareness level among large companies was twice that of SMEs. Among the companies that were aware of CSR, about two-thirds have implemented CSR in areas such as sustainable development, fair employment, and corporate philanthropy. Their main motivations were corporate culture and to improve branding. The other one-third, who did not implement CSR, felt that it was not relevant to their business or lacked the funding and training resources. The Singapore Stock Exchange implemented a requirement in June 2011 that listed companies report on their sustainable business practices.

Political Violence

Singapore's political environment is stable and there is no history of incidents involving politically motivated damage to foreign investments in Singapore. The ruling People's Action Party (PAP) has dominated Singapore's parliamentary government since 1959, and currently controls 80 of the 87 regularly contested parliamentary seats. Singapore opposition parties, which currently hold seven regularly contested parliamentary seats and three additional seats reserved to the opposition by the constitution, do not usually espouse views that are radically different from the mainstream of Singapore political opinion.

Corruption

Corruption, including bribery, raises the costs and risks of doing business. Corruption has a corrosive impact on both market opportunities overseas for U.S. companies and the broader business climate. It also deters international investment, stifles economic growth and development, distorts prices, and undermines the rule of law.

It is important for U.S. companies, irrespective of their size, to assess the business climate in the relevant market in which they will be operating or investing, and to have an effective compliance program or measures to prevent and detect corruption, including foreign bribery. U.S. individuals and firms operating or investing in foreign markets should take the time to become familiar with the relevant anticorruption laws of both the foreign country and the United States in order to properly comply with them, and where appropriate, they should seek the advice of legal counsel.

The U.S. Government seeks to level the global playing field for U.S. businesses by encouraging other countries to take steps to criminalize their own companies' acts of corruption, including bribery of foreign public officials, by requiring them to uphold their obligations under relevant international conventions. A U. S. firm that believes a competitor is seeking to use bribery of a foreign public official to secure a contract should bring this to the attention of appropriate U.S. agencies, as noted below.

U.S. Foreign Corrupt Practices Act: In 1977, the United States enacted the Foreign Corrupt Practices Act (FCPA), which makes it unlawful for a U.S. person, and certain foreign issuers of securities, to make a corrupt payment to foreign public officials for the purpose of obtaining or retaining business for or with, or directing business to, any person. The FCPA also applies to foreign firms and persons who take any act in furtherance of such a corrupt payment while in the United States. For more detailed information on the FCPA, see the FCPA Lay-Person's Guide at: http://www.justice.gov/criminal/fraud/

Other Instruments: It is U.S. Government policy to promote good governance, including host country implementation and enforcement of anti-corruption laws and policies pursuant to their obligations under international agreements. Since enactment of the FCPA, the United States has been instrumental to the expansion of the international framework to fight corruption. Several significant components of this framework are the OECD Convention on Combating Bribery of Foreign Public Officials in International Business Transactions (OECD Antibribery Convention), the United Nations Convention against Corruption (UN Convention), the Inter-American Convention against Corruption (OAS Convention), the Council of Europe Criminal and Civil Law Conventions, and a growing list of U.S. free trade agreements. This country is party to [add instrument to which this country is party], but generally all countries prohibit the bribery and solicitation of their public officials.

OECD Antibribery Convention: The OECD Antibribery Convention entered into force in February 1999. As of March 2009, there are 38 parties to the Convention including the United States (see http://www.oecd.org/dataoecd/59/13/40272933.pdf). Major exporters China, India, and Russia are not parties, although the U.S. Government strongly endorses their eventual accession to the Convention. The Convention obligates the Parties to criminalize bribery of foreign public officials in the conduct of international business. The United States meets its international obligations under the OECD Antibribery Convention through the U.S. FCPA. Singapore is not a party to the OECD Convention on Combating Bribery.

UN Convention: The UN Anticorruption Convention entered into force on December 14, 2005, and there are 158 parties to it as of November 2011 (see http://www.unodc.org/unodc/en/treaties/CAC/signatories.html). The UN Convention is the first global comprehensive international anticorruption agreement. The UN

Convention requires countries to establish criminal and other offences to cover a wide range of acts of corruption. The UN Convention goes beyond previous anticorruption instruments, covering a broad range of issues ranging from basic forms of corruption such as bribery and solicitation, embezzlement, trading in influence to the concealment and laundering of the proceeds of corruption. The Convention contains transnational business bribery provisions that are functionally similar to those in the OECD Antibribery Convention and contains provisions on private sector auditing and books and records requirements. Other provisions address matters such as prevention, international cooperation, and asset recovery. Singapore is a party to the UN Convention.

OAS Convention: In 1996, the Member States of the Organization of American States (OAS) adopted the first international anticorruption legal instrument, the Inter-American Convention against Corruption (OAS Convention), which entered into force in March 1997. The OAS Convention, among other things, establishes a set of preventive measures against corruption provides for the criminalization of certain acts of corruption, including transnational bribery and illicit enrichment, and contains a series of provisions to strengthen the cooperation between its States Parties in areas such as mutual legal assistance and technical cooperation. As of December 2009, the OAS Convention has 34 parties (see http://www.oas.org/juridico/english/Sigs/b-58.html) Singapore is not a party to the OAS Convention.

Council of Europe Criminal Law and Civil Law Conventions: Many European countries are parties to either the Council of Europe (CoE) Criminal Law Convention on Corruption, the Civil Law Convention, or both. The Criminal Law Convention requires criminalization of a wide range of national and transnational conduct, including bribery, money-laundering, and account offenses. It also incorporates provisions on liability of legal persons and witness protection. The Civil Law Convention includes provisions on compensation for damage relating to corrupt acts, whistleblower protection, and validity of contracts, inter alia. The Group of States against Corruption (GRECO) was established in 1999 by the CoE to monitor compliance with these and related anti-corruption standards. Currently, GRECO comprises 49 member States (48 European countries and the United States). As of December 2011, the Criminal Law Convention has 43 parties and the Civil Law Convention has 34 (see www.coe.int/greco.) Singapore is not a party to the Council of Europe Conventions.

Free Trade Agreements: While it is U.S. Government policy to include anticorruption provisions in free trade agreements (FTAs) that it negotiates with its trading partners, the anticorruption provisions have evolved over time. The most recent FTAs negotiated now require trading partners to criminalize "active bribery" of public officials (offering bribes to any public official must be made a criminal offense, both domestically and trans-nationally) as well as domestic "passive bribery" (solicitation of a bribe by a domestic official). All U.S. FTAs may be found at the U.S. Trade Representative Website: http://www.ustr.gov/trade-agreements/free-trade-agreements. Singapore has a free trade agreement (FTA) in place with the United States, the U.S. – Singapore FTA, which came into force on January 1, 2004.

Local Laws: U.S. firms should familiarize themselves with local anticorruption laws, and, where appropriate, seek legal counsel. While the U.S. Department of Commerce cannot provide legal advice on local laws, the Department's U.S. and Foreign Commercial Service can provide assistance with navigating the host country's legal system and obtaining a list of local legal counsel.

Assistance for U.S. Businesses: The U.S. Department of Commerce offers several services to aid U.S. businesses seeking to address business-related corruption issues. For example, the U.S. and Foreign Commercial Service can provide services that may assist U.S. companies in conducting their due diligence as part of the company's overarching compliance program when choosing business partners or agents overseas. The U.S. Foreign and Commercial Service can be reached directly through its offices in every major U.S. and foreign city, or through its Website at www.trade.gov/cs.

The Departments of Commerce and State provide worldwide support for qualified U.S. companies bidding on foreign government contracts through the Commerce Department's Advocacy Center and State's Office of Commercial and Business Affairs. Problems, including alleged corruption by foreign governments or competitors, encountered by U.S. companies in seeking such foreign business opportunities can be brought to the attention of appropriate U.S. government officials, including local embassy personnel and through the Department of Commerce Trade Compliance Center "Report A Trade Barrier" Website at tcc.export.gov/Report_a_Barrier/index.asp.

Guidance on the U.S. FCPA: The Department of Justice's (DOJ) FCPA Opinion Procedure enables U.S. firms and individuals to request a statement of the Justice Department's present enforcement intentions under the anti-bribery provisions of the FCPA regarding any proposed business conduct. The details of the opinion procedure are available on DOJ's Fraud Section Website at www.justice.gov/criminal/fraud/fcpa. Although the Department of Commerce has no enforcement role with respect to the FCPA, it supplies general guidance to U.S. exporters who have questions about the FCPA and about international developments concerning the FCPA. For further information, see the Office of the Chief Counsel for International Counsel, U.S. Department of Commerce, Website, at http://www.ogc.doc.gov/trans_anti_bribery.html. More general information on the FCPA is available at the Websites listed below.

Exporters and investors should be aware that generally all countries prohibit the bribery of their public officials, and prohibit their officials from soliciting bribes under domestic laws. Most countries are required to criminalize such bribery and other acts of corruption by virtue of being parties to various international conventions discussed above.

Singapore typically ranks as the least corrupt country in Asia and one of the least corrupt in the world. For years Singapore was number one (i.e., least corrupt) on watchdog group Transparency International (TI)'s global index, but due to TI's new ranking methodology starting 2011, Singapore is now fifth. TI has said the lower ranking is statistically insignificant and does not indicate increased corruption in Singapore.

Singapore actively enforces its strong anti-corruption laws. The Prevention of Corruption Act, and the Drug Trafficking and Other Serious Crimes (Confiscation of Benefits) Act provide the legal basis for government action by the Corrupt Practices Investigation Bureau, an anti-corruption agency that reports to the Prime Minister. These laws cover acts of corruption both within Singapore as well as those committed by Singaporeans abroad. When cases of corruption are uncovered, whether in the public or private sector, the government deals with them firmly, swiftly and publicly, as they do in cases where public officials are involved in dishonest and illegal behavior.

Singapore is not a party to the OECD Convention on Combating Bribery, but the Prevention of Corruption Act makes it a crime for a Singapore citizen to bribe a foreign official or any other person, whether within or outside Singapore.

Anti-Corruption Resources

Some useful resources for individuals and companies regarding combating corruption in global markets include the following:

- Information about the U.S. Foreign Corrupt Practices Act (FCPA), including a "Lay-Person's Guide to the FCPA" is available at the U.S. Department of Justice's Website at: http://www.justice.gov/criminal/fraud/fcpa.

- Information about the OECD Antibribery Convention including links to national implementing legislation and country monitoring reports is available at: http://www.oecd.org/department/0,3355,en_2649_34859_1_1_1_1_1,00.html. See also new Antibribery Recommendation and Good Practice Guidance Annex for companies: http://www.oecd.org/dataoecd/11/40/44176910.pdf.

- General information about anticorruption initiatives, such as the OECD Convention and the FCPA, including translations of the statute into several languages, is available at the Department of Commerce Office of the Chief Counsel for International Commerce Website: http://www.ogc.doc.gov/trans_anti_bribery.html.

- Transparency International (TI) publishes an annual Corruption Perceptions Index (CPI). The CPI measures the perceived level of public-sector corruption in 180 countries and territories around the world. The CPI is available at: http://www.transparency.org/policy_research/surveys_indices/cpi/2009. TI also publishes an annual *Global Corruption Report* which provides a systematic evaluation of the state of corruption around the world. It includes an in-depth analysis of a focal theme, a series of country reports that document major corruption related events and developments from all continents and an overview of the latest research findings on anti-corruption diagnostics and tools. See http://www.transparency.org/publications/gcr.

- The World Bank Institute publishes Worldwide Governance Indicators (WGI). These indicators assess six dimensions of governance in 213 countries, including Voice and Accountability, Political Stability and Absence of Violence, Government Effectiveness, Regulatory Quality, Rule of Law and Control of Corruption. See http://info.worldbank.org/governance/wgi/index.asp. The World Bank Business Environment and Enterprise Performance Surveys may also be of interest and are available at: http://data.worldbank.org/data-catalog/BEEPS.

- The World Economic Forum publishes the *Global Enabling Trade Report*, which presents the rankings of the Enabling Trade Index, and includes an assessment of the transparency of border administration (focused on bribe payments and corruption) and a separate segment on corruption and the regulatory environment. See http://www.weforum.org/s?s=global+enabling+trade+report.

- Additional country information related to corruption can be found in the U.S. State Department's annual Human Rights Report available at http://www.state.gov/g/drl/rls/hrrpt/.

- Global Integrity, a nonprofit organization, publishes its annual *Global Integrity Report*, which provides indicators for 106 countries with respect to governance and anti-corruption. The report highlights the strengths and weaknesses of national level anti-corruption systems. The report is available at: http://report.globalintegrity.org/.

Bilateral Investment Agreements   Return to top

Singapore has signed Investment Guarantee Agreements (IGA's) with 41 countries, including the United States. These agreements mutually protect nationals or companies of either country against war and non-commercial risks of expropriation and nationalization.

Singapore has signed free trade agreements that include investment chapters with Australia, China, the European Free Trade Area (Switzerland, Norway, Lichtenstein, and Iceland), the Gulf Cooperation Council (comprising Bahrain, Kuwait, Oman, Qatar, Saudi Arabia and the United Arab Emirates), India, Japan, Jordan, New Zealand, Panama, Peru, South Korea, Costa Rica, European Union, Taiwan, and the United States. Singapore is negotiating FTAs with Canada, Mexico, Pakistan, Turkey, and Ukraine. Singapore is a member of the Association of Southeast Asian Nations (ASEAN), which has concluded FTAs with Australia and New Zealand, China, India, and South Korea, and a Comprehensive Economic Partnership Agreement with Japan. Singapore is also a party in the Transpacific Strategic Economic Partnership Agreement together with Chile, New Zealand, and Brunei. These four nations formed the basis for the Trans-Pacific Partnership, a multi-lateral free trade agreement currently in negotiations that now includes Singapore, the U.S. and ten other countries (Australia, Brunei Darussalam, Canada, Chile, Malaysia, Mexico, New Zealand, Peru, Japan and Viet Nam). Singapore is also leading the goods chapter's negotiations for the Regional Comprehensive Economic Partnership (RCEP) FTA which was launched in November 2012 and includes ASEAN members plus Australia, China, India, Japan, New Zealand, and South Korea. Singapore has signed Comprehensive Avoidance of Double Taxation Agreements with a number of countries, but not with the United States.

OPIC and Other Investment Insurance Programs   Return to top

Under the 1966 Investment Guarantee Agreement with Singapore, the U.S. Overseas Private Investment Corporation (OPIC) offers insurance to U.S. investors in Singapore against currency inconvertibility, expropriation, and losses arising from war. Singapore became a member of the Multilateral Investment Guarantee Agency (MIGA) in 1998.

Labor   Return to top

As of mid-2013, Singapore's labor market totaled 3.44 million workers; this includes about 1.30 million foreigners, of which about 85 percent are unskilled or semi-skilled workers. Local labor laws are flexible, and allow for relatively free hiring and firing practices. Either party can terminate employment by giving the other party the required notice. The Ministry of Manpower (MOM) must approve employment of foreigners. Since

2011 the Government has introduced policy measures to support productivity increases coupled with reduced dependence on foreign labor. The MOM has started tightening foreign labor approvals, resulting in many businesses in Singapore voicing discontent at not being able to access sufficient labor.

In order to tackle the growing concerns that many foreigners are displacing locals in the job market, as well as concerns that many foreign managers are hiring their own fellow countryman instead of recruiting based on merit, Singapore's Ministry on Manpower (MOM) announced a ruling in September 2013, requiring employers to consider Singaporeans fairly, before hiring skilled professional foreigners. The new rules, known as the Fair Consideration Framework (FCF) will be implemented from August 2014 and affect employers who apply for Employment Passes (EP), the work pass for foreign professionals working in professional, manager and executive (PME) posts. Under the new rules, firms making new EP applications must first advertise the job vacancy in a new jobs bank administered by the Singapore Workforce and Development Agency (WDA) for at least 14 days. The jobs bank will be free for use by companies and job seekers and the job advertisement must be open to all Singaporeans. Employers are encouraged to keep records of their interview process as proof that they have done due diligence in trying to look for a Singaporean worker. If an EP is still needed, the employer will have to make a statutory declaration that a job advertisement with the national jobs bank had been made. Some exceptions have been made for smaller firms with 25 or fewer employees and jobs which pay a fixed monthly salary of $9,600 (S$12,000) or more will not be subjected to the advertising requirement. Consistent with Singapore's WTO obligations, intra-corporate transfers (ICT) are allowed for managers, executives, and specialists who had worked for at least one-year in the firm before being posted to Singapore. ICT would still be required to meet all EP criteria, but the requirement for an advertisement in the jobs data bank would be waived.

Singapore imposes a ceiling on the ratio of unskilled/semi-skilled foreign workers to local workers that a company can employ, and charges a monthly levy for each unskilled or semi-skilled foreign worker. The government also provides incentives and assistance to firms to automate and invest in labor-saving technology.

Labor-management relations in Singapore are generally amicable. Slightly over 20 percent of the workforce is unionized. The majority of unions are affiliated with the National Trades Union Congress (NTUC), which maintains a symbiotic relationship with the PAP ruling party. Although workers, other than those employed in the three essential services of water, gas and electricity, have the legal right to strike, no workers did so between 1986-2011. In November 2012, some 171 SMRT bus drivers from China held an illegal strike. The drivers complained about poor living conditions and lower wages compared to Malaysian drivers. The incident resulted in a total of 4 Chinese drivers being charged in Singapore court for instigating the strike and another 29 Chinese SMRT bus drivers having their work permits revoked and being sent home. In February 2013, the 4 former SMRT bus drivers from China plead guilty and received jail terms of between six and seven weeks for instigating an illegal strike in November 2012 that caused inconvenience to the public. Singapore has no minimum wage law; the government follows a policy of allowing free market forces to determine wage levels. Singapore has a flexible wage system in which the National Wage Council (NWC) recommends non-binding wage adjustments on an annual basis. The NWC is a tripartite body comprising a Chairman and representatives from the Government, employers and unions. The NWC recommendations apply to all employees in both domestic and foreign firms, and across the private and public sectors. While the NWC wage guidelines are not mandatory, they are widely implemented. The level of implementation is generally higher among unionized companies compared to non-unionized companies.

Foreign-Trade Zones/Free Ports   Return to top

Singapore has eight free-trade zones (FTZs), six for seaborne cargo and two for airfreight. The FTZs may be used for storage and repackaging of import and export cargo, and goods transiting Singapore for subsequent re-export. Manufacturing is not carried out within the zones. Foreign and local firms have equal access to the FTZ facilities.

Foreign Direct Investment Statistics   Return to top

The United States is one of Singapore's largest foreign investors, with more than an estimated 3,000 U.S. firms in operation. According to the Singapore Department of Statistics (Singapore DOS), U.S. cumulative foreign direct investments in Singapore totaled US$85.99 billion in 2012 (latest available data). According to U.S. Department of Commerce statistics (USDOC), U.S. firms (manufacturing and services) in 2012 had cumulative total investments in Singapore of $138.6 billion. Discrepancies between USG and GOS FDI numbers are attributable to differences in accounting methodologies.

TABLE A
STOCK OF FOREIGN DIRECT INVESTMENT (FDI) IN SINGAPORE BY COUNTRY
(As at Year-end, Historical Cost)
(US$ million)

	2008	2009	2010	2011
Total	360,698.33	395,158.34	461,874.37	534,238.97
Asia	84,778.70	100,220.49	112,432.20	128,736.86
Brunei Darussalam	209.92	218.56	214.52	270.69
Cambodia	1.06	0.62	5.06	17.49
China	3,126.73	6,686.63	10,480.31	11,706.73
Hong Kong	8,430.24	12,475.63	13,631.90	18,662.29
India	11,917.87	15,094.40	17,975.28	18,925.35
Indonesia	2,093.86	2,677.21	1,114.12	1,073.30
Israel	3,577.04	3,432.45	3,455.01	3,773.83

Japan	35,455.89	34,645.24	39,418.70	41,764.77
Korea, Republic of	2,297.36	1,998.14	2,703.70	3,306.62
Lao People's Democratic Republic	1.13	3.92	1.83	7.00
Malaysia	8,895.32	10,907.25	10,517.79	14,803.40
Myanmar	66.94	12.99	44.00	25.60
Philippines	778.20	742.73	946.46	937.99
Taiwan	4,631.89	4,241.60	4,222.74	5,812.39
Thailand	1,282.37	1,427.29	3,929.52	3,177.36
Vietnam	20.43	19.39	43.71	47.62
Europe	**144,092.24**	**152,773.94**	**170,250.09**	**200,333.25**
Denmark	2,192.18	2,684.77	6,081.26	6,985.29
France	6,719.82	5,571.47	5,933.33	8,141.82
Germany	7,935.40	7,656.51	10,240.12	10,308.21
Ireland	2,322.66	2,125.89	3,762.52	5,584.07
Netherlands	43,116.62	42,210.66	44,303.12	52,719.45
Norway	15,031.81	15,905.12	16,113.90	17,302.89
Switzerland	16,613.58	18,460.98	20,220.02	22,858.97
United Kingdom	35,391.57	34,031.90	36,723.07	44,426.82
United States	37,440.20	40,427.84	49,886.69	61,961.60
Canada	2,136.06	1,981.51	2,525.05	2,923.84
Australia	3,232.05	4,124.85	6,740.45	7,833.77
New Zealand	1,344.78	1,450.40	2,147.85	2,448.21
South and Central America and the	**76,864.08**	**83,712.20**	**105,086.91**	**116,288.74**

Caribbean				
Africa	8,711.83	8,788.11	11,409.83	11,826.77

Source: Department of Statistics, "Foreign Equity Investment in Singapore, 2011"

TABLE B
STOCK OF DIRECT INVESTMENT ABROAD BY COUNTRY
(As at Year-end, Historical Cost)
(US$ Million)

	2008	2009	2010	2011
Total	**220,550.1**	**253,478.2**	**312,622.3**	**356,917.9**
Asia	**124,472.8**	**137,825.2**	**166,315.2**	**206,883.5**
Brunei Darussalam	113.1	138.9	130.3	121.9
Cambodia	189.6	186.9	199.1	186.4
China	38,504.1	41,663.1	50,745.9	65,268.0
Hong Kong	14,174.7	16,105.3	18,341.0	30,599.7
India	4,764.6	6,562.5	8,479.4	9,199.3
Indonesia	15,781.1	17,817.9	20,891.5	26,572.0
Japan	5,682.6	6,455.0	9,950.1	12,342.5
Korea, Republic of	1,788.8	1,915.4	2,362.6	2,672.4
Lao, People's Democratic Republic	150.1	155.6	163.3	179.0
Malaysia	17,244.9	18,980.3	23,471.0	27,299.7
Myanmar	877.8	1,521.6	4,152.8	3,499.3
Philippines	3,033.4	3,422.8	3,840.0	4,286.9
Taiwan	4,199.8	4,124.6	4,283.2	4,664.4
Thailand	13,575.0	14,048.3	14,654.5	15,182.7
Vietnam	2,005.2	2,152.8	2,003.2	2,279.4
Europe	**26,236.1**	**35,050.3**	**46,302.5**	**49,132.4**
Germany	419.4	686.2	1,258.2	1,509.4
Netherlands	3,051.6	3,418.6	5,501.9	5,459.5
Norway	1,225.8	1,348.5	1,558.9	2,207.3
Switzerland	3,359.2	3,257.7	3,251.4	2,668.7
United Kingdom	14,012.8	22,242.5	28,971.3	29,509.1
United States	8,295.0	9,030.3	10,378.7	6,058.1
Canada	44.8	575.2	385.8	661.7
Australia	12,808.6	15,886.3	24,439.0	28,172.7
New Zealand	653.1	769.6	928.1	1,181.3
South and Central America	**37,264.2**	**40,182.7**	**43,173.6**	**45,202.9**

and the Caribbean				
Africa	9,270.9	12,684.0	18,992.8	17,590.1

Source: Department of Statistics, "Singapore Direct Investment Abroad, 2011"

TABLE C
GDP AND FDI FIGURES, 2006-2011
(US$ Million)

Year	GDP*	FDI	FDI as ratio to GDP
2006	145,639.9	233,176.9	1.60
2007	177,866.2	309,579.6	1.74
2008	190,598.0	360,698.3	1.89
2009	188,831.4	395158.3	2.09
2010	231,698.7	461874.4	1.99
2011	265,595.6	534239.0	2.01

Footnote: *GDP at Current Market Price
Source: Department of Statistics

Web Resources   Return to top

http://www.mas.gov.sg/Singapore-Financial-Centre/Value-Propositions/Setting-Up.aspx
http://www.wipo.int/about-wipo/en/offices/singapore/
http://www.reach.gov.sg
https://licences.business.gov.sg

Return to table of contents

Return to table of contents

Chapter 7: Trade and Project Financing

- How Do I Get Paid (Methods of Payment)
- How Does the Banking System Operate
- Foreign-Exchange Controls
- U.S. Banks and Local Correspondent Banks
- Project Financing
- Web Resources

How Do I Get Paid (Methods of Payment)   Return to top

Singapore has a well-developed financial system, which offers a full range of export finance instruments. Shipments are generally made under letters of credit and sight drafts (or bills of exchange), depending on the exporter's preference and the extent of past dealings with the purchaser. Standard credit terms are generally 30 to 90 days and they are allocated on market terms. Quotations are generally made on a C.I.F. basis. Prices given in U.S. dollars should be clearly stated to avoid confusion with the Singapore dollar. Exporters making quotations in Singapore dollars should consult their banks for the prevailing exchange rate. Singapore uses the metric system, so it is beneficial for price/quantity quotations to be prepared accordingly.

How Does the Banking System Operate   Return to top

Singapore is a reputable international financial center. It is a leading world foreign exchange trading center and trader in derivatives. There are about 900 local and foreign banking and financial institutions in Singapore that provide services relating to trade financing, foreign exchange, derivatives products, capital markets activities, loan syndication, underwriting, mergers and acquisitions, asset management, securities trading, financial advisory services and specialized insurance services.

The Monetary Authority of Singapore (MAS) performs all the functions of a central bank including the issuance of currency. The unit of legal tender is the Singapore dollar. The MAS is a wholly owned and controlled statutory board under the Ministry of Finance; it is responsible for all matters relating to banks and financial institutions. Besides regulating financial institutions, the MAS has a Financial Sector Promotion Department that promotes new financial activities, develops IT infrastructure and manpower resources for the financial sector, and designs appropriate incentives to attract international financial firms to conduct activities in Singapore.

In October 2005, Singapore enacted the Deposit Insurance Act and the deposit insurance program took effect from April 1, 2006. In the event that a bank or finance company fails, the program compensates individuals and charities for the first S$20,000 (about US$15,750) of their Singapore dollar deposits in standard savings, current and fixed deposit accounts, net of liabilities. The program compensates depositors through a fund built up from contributions by full banks and finance companies. For deposits in excess of the payout, individual depositors can also claim from assets of the failed bank. Depositors and policyholders, in the case of an insurance company, would rank ahead of unsecured creditors and shareholders in their claims. The MAS, together with the Singapore Deposit Insurance Corporation (SDIC) that administers the deposit insurance program, will review the coverage limit regularly, taking into consideration the objectives of the program and international norms.

The MAS is known and respected as an effective regulator/supervisor of the financial services sector. MAS will require Singapore-incorporated banks to meet a minimum Common Equity Tier 1 ("CET1") capital adequacy ratio ("CAR") of 6.5%, Tier 1 CAR of 8% and Total CAR of 10% from 1 January 2015. These standards (http://www.mas.gov.sg/news-and-publications/press-releases/2011/mas-strengthens-capital-requirements-for-singapore-incorporated-banks.aspx) are higher than the Basel III minimum requirements of 4.5%, 6% and 8% for CET1 CAR, Tier 1 CAR and Total CAR, respectively. Financial statements are in compliance with international standards and internationally recognized accounting firms perform audits. In December 2013, total assets/liabilities of Singapore's domestic banking sector amounted to almost US$567 billion, which is a 12% increase from the previous year.

Foreign-Exchange Controls Return to top

Singapore has no significant restrictions on remittances, foreign exchange transactions and capital movements. It also does not restrict reinvestment or repatriation of earnings and capital. In addition, The U.S.-Singapore FTA underpins the shared commitment of the United States and Singapore to the free transfer of capital, unimpeded by regulatory restrictions.

U.S. Banks and Local Correspondent Banks Return to top

As of April 2014, there were 28 foreign full service licensees, 55 wholesale licensees, and 36 offshore licensees operating in Singapore. Of the 28 foreign full service licensees, the government has granted "qualifying full bank" (QFB) licenses to ten foreign banks, one of which is Citibank Singapore. Except in retail banking, Singapore laws do not distinguish operationally between foreign and domestic banks. The four U.S. banks with a license to provide full banking services are: Bank of America N.A., Citibank N.A., Citibank Singapore Limited, and JPMorgan Chase Bank N.A. The MAS maintains a full directory of local and foreign banks and financial institutions (including U.S.-headquartered entities) that operate in Singapore. Access to this directory is free and is available at the following website: https://secure.mas.gov.sg/fid/

Project Financing Return to top

Singapore is considered a developed country and does not receive development assistance from multilateral institutions. U.S. government agencies such as the Export-Import Bank of the United States and the U.S. Department of Agriculture, OPIC, as well as state and local bodies (e.g., Small Business Administration) offer a variety of programs to assist exporters with their financing and insurance needs. Firms seeking such assistance should contact their nearest Export Assistance Center (http://www.export.gov/comm_svc/eac.html).

Web Resources Return to top

Export-Import Bank of the United States: http://www.exim.gov

Country Limitation Schedule: http://www.exim.gov/tools/country/country_limits.html

OPIC: http://www.opic.gov

Trade and Development Agency: http://www.tda.gov/

SBA's Office of International Trade: http://www.sba.gov/oit/

USDA Commodity Credit Corporation: http://www.fsa.usda.gov/ccc/default.htm

U.S. Agency for International Development: http://www.usaid.gov

Return to table of contents

Return to table of contents

Chapter 8: Business Travel

- Business Customs
- Travel Advisory
- Visa Requirements
- Telecommunications
- Transportation
- Language
- Health
- Local Time, Business Hours and Holidays
- Temporary Entry of Materials and Personal Belongings
- Web Resources

Business Customs   Return to top

Business discussions are usually conducted in a very straightforward manner. English is widely spoken and most businesspeople are skilled and technically knowledgeable. Most agents/distributors have visited the United States and often handle several American product lines. Corruption is virtually non-existent.

Many Singapore business people are of ethnic Chinese background, and many of them will have "Western" first names (e.g., Nancy Goh). Those who do not will have only their Chinese name on their business card, in which case the family name is listed first. Mr. Chan Yiu Kei would be addressed as "Mr. Chan" and Ms. Wong Ai Lan as "Ms. Wong."

The names of business people of Malay or Indian descent are written and spoken as given name followed by family name. For the sake of politeness and respect, it is wise to address a businessperson by the last name rather than the first name until invited to use a given name. When in doubt it is not impolite to ask. The common and polite Singaporean phrase is 'How shall I address you?'

Business cards are a must as they are immediately exchanged during business and social meetings. The East Asian practice of presenting a business card with both hands is observed. There is no need to have special business cards printed in Chinese.

Located a few degrees from the Equator, Singapore has a constant tropical climate year-round. Daytime temperatures average between 85 and 90 degrees Fahrenheit. Humidity is very high and rain showers are frequent. Temperatures at night average between 76 and 80 degrees. All public buildings, indoor restaurants and taxis are air-conditioned.

Summer-weight suits/dresses, several dress-shirts, and an umbrella are recommended for the traveler. Singapore business dress is a long-sleeved shirt and tie for men, although one will not be out of place without a tie. Some formal meetings call for a coat and tie. Businesswomen wear light-weight attire. Evening dinner-dress is a shirt and tie for men but there isn't a strict dress code for women.

Tipping is not customary in Singapore. Restaurants automatically add a 10% service charge and a 7% goods and services tax (GST) to the bill. Singapore's unit of currency is the Singapore dollar. Travelers' checks and currency may be exchanged in the baggage claim area at Changi Airport (at a reasonable rate) or at any hotel (at a less favorable rate). Singapore features dozens of Government-authorized "money changers" located in major shopping centers, offering competitive rates and they will usually accept U.S. travelers' checks as well as major currencies. International credit cards are widely accepted in hotels, restaurants and retail shops. ATMs that accept U.S. cards are widely available.

Travel Advisory   Return to top

Americans traveling abroad should regularly monitor the Department of State's, Bureau of Consular Affairs' web site at http://travel.state.gov/, where the current Travel Warnings and Travel Alerts, as well as the Worldwide Caution, can be found.

The Department of State urges American citizens to take responsibility for their own personal security while traveling overseas. For general information about appropriate measures travelers can take to protect themselves in an overseas environment, see the Department of State's pamphlet A Safe Trip Abroad.
(http://travel.state.gov/travel/tips/safety/safety_1747.html)

While in a foreign country, a U.S. citizen is subject to that country's laws and regulations, which sometimes differ significantly from those in the United States and may not afford the protections available to the individual under U.S. law. Penalties for breaking the law can be more severe than those in the United States for similar offenses. Persons violating Singapore laws, even unknowingly, may be expelled, arrested or imprisoned.

There are strict penalties for possession and use of drugs as well as for trafficking in illegal drugs. Visitors should be aware of Singapore's strict laws and penalties for a variety of actions that might not be illegal or might be considered minor offenses in the United States. Commercial disputes that may be handled as civil suits in the United States can escalate to criminal cases in Singapore and may result in heavy fines and prison sentences.

Singapore customs authorities enforce strict regulations concerning temporary import and export of items such as weapons, illegal drugs, certain religious materials and pornographic material. Singapore customs authorities' definition of "weapon" is very broad, and, in addition to firearms, includes many items which are not necessarily seen as weapons in the United States, such as dive knives, kitchen knives, handcuffs and expended shell casings. Carrying any of these items without permission may result in immediate arrest. All baggage is x-rayed at every port of entry, so checked baggage will also be inspected for regulated items.

Generally, there are four types of dutiable goods in Singapore: alcoholic beverages, tobacco, gasoline and motor vehicles. Travelers entering Singapore at any port of entry must approach an Immigration and Checkpoints Authority (ICA) officer at the "Red Channel" for payment of duty (e.g. alcohol and tobacco) and goods and services tax (GST) if you have dutiable goods which exceed the GST relief or duty-free concession.

It is an offence to proceed to the "Green Channel" for clearance if you have items that are subject to payment of duty and/or GST.

The State Department Consular Information Sheet on Singapore can be found at: http://travel.state.gov/content/passports/english/country/singapore.html.

Visa Requirements   Return to top

U.S. citizens do not need a visa if their visit to Singapore is for business or social purposes and their stay is for 90 days or less. Travelers to the region should note that Singapore and some neighboring countries do not allow Americans to enter under any circumstances with fewer than six months of validity remaining on their passport. Travelers should note that there are also very strict penalties for overstaying their visas.

Specific information about entry requirements for Singapore may be obtained from the Embassy of the Republic of Singapore (http://www.mfa.gov.sg/washington/).

U.S. companies should note that Singapore is part of the Visa Waiver Program and that eligible nationals of Singapore are able to travel to the United States without a visa for tourist and business travel of 90 days or less provided they possess an e-passport and an approved authorization through the Electronic System for Travel Authorization (ESTA). Third country nationals living and working in Singapore may have to obtain a visa before visiting the United States. U.S. Companies that require travel of foreign businesspersons to the United States should be advised that security evaluations are handled via an interagency process. Visa applicants should go to the following links:

State Department Visa Website: http://travel.state.gov/content/visas/english.html

U.S. Embassy, Singapore: http://singapore.usembassy.gov/

ESTA: https://esta.cbp.dhs.gov

Telecommunications   Return to top

Telecommunications and Internet facilities in Singapore are state-of-the-art, providing high-quality communications with the rest of the world. Mobile phone users can access third generation (3G) and 4G or Long Term Evolution (LTE) networks and services in Singapore, with theoretical speeds of up to 150 Megabits per second (Mbps). Internet connections are widely available in hotels.

There are three main mobile telephony providers (and 15 mobile virtual network operators or MVNOs) and 104 Internet Services Providers in Singapore. The mobile penetration rate is close to 156% in December 2013. Household broadband penetration is at 105% as of December 2013.

Singapore's island-wide free Wi-Fi service offers additional connectivity options. Called Wireless@SG, it offers access speeds of up to 2Mbp at over 5,000 Wi-Fi hot spots in public places such as shopping malls, town centers and the business district. Visitors with foreign SIM cards can also register for a free account at any Wireless@SG hotspot and receive their login details through SMS messages sent to their foreign mobile numbers. Alternatively, visitors can buy a local prepaid SIM card from mobile operators M1 and StarHub to log on to Wireless@SG via a SIM-based login feature.

All homes and offices now have access to the new, ultra high-speed, all-fiber Nationwide Broadband Network (NBN). Offering pervasive, competitively priced broadband speeds, the NBN enables users to enjoy a richer broadband experience at comparable prices to ADSL and cable connection. Enterprises, large and small, also benefit from the ease of access to ultra high-speed broadband of up to 10Gbps, and are able to use infocomm more extensively to boost productivity and competitiveness.

Besides a nationwide broadband network infrastructure, Singapore is well connected by multiple satellite and submarine cable systems with more than 183.4 terabits per second (Tbps) of potential capacity supporting international and regional telecoms connectivity. It has more than 2.98 terabits per second (Tbps) of international internet bandwidth connectivity to economies such as the US, China, Japan, India, as well as some countries in Europe and ASEAN.

Transportation

Situated at the crossroads of international shipping and air routes, Singapore is a center for transportation and communication in Southeast Asia. With more than 90 airlines serving over 200 cities, Singapore's Changi Airport has established itself as a major aviation hub in the Asia Pacific region. Singapore is also a leading international maritime center, home to more than 120 international shipping groups. In 2013, Singapore was the second busiest container port in the world handling 32.24 million Twenty-Foot Equivalent Units (TEUs). The country is linked by road and rail to Malaysia.

Taxis are abundant, metered, safe, inexpensive and air-conditioned, and most drivers speak English. Drivers should be given place names for the destination as these are often more familiar than street names. Traffic flow is good. The Government limits the total number of cars on the road through heavy fees/taxes and imposes a surcharge on vehicles entering the Central Business District during peak hours. In addition, an exceptionally clean, efficient subway system links the major business/shopping areas.

Language

English is widely spoken in Singapore. It is the language of business, government, education and the media. Many business people are highly educated and have traveled extensively.

Health

Good medical care is widely available in Singapore and high-end medical tourism is a growing business. Doctors and hospitals expect immediate payment for health services by credit card or cash and generally do not accept U.S. health insurance. Recipients of health care should be aware that the Ministry of Health auditors in certain circumstances may be granted access to patient medical records without the consent of the patient, and in certain circumstances, physicians may be required to provide information relating to the diagnosis or treatment without the patient's consent.

MEDICAL INSURANCE: The Department of State strongly urges Americans to consult with their medical insurance company prior to traveling abroad to confirm whether their policy applies overseas and whether it will cover emergency expenses such as a medical evacuation. Please see information on medical insurance overseas.

OTHER HEALTH INFORMATION: Information on vaccinations and other health precautions may be obtained from the Centers for Disease Control and Prevention's automated information line for international travelers at 877-FYI-TRIP (877-394-8747) or via http://wwwn.cdc.gov/travel/default.aspx. For information about outbreaks of infectious diseases abroad consult the World Health Organization's website at http://www.who.int/en. The World Health Organization also provides additional health information at http://www.who.int/ith. The Singapore Ministry of Health's web site, http://www.moh.gov.sg/, contains helpful health information.

Local Time, Business Hours, and Holidays   Return to top

Singapore is twelve hours ahead of Eastern Daylight Savings or thirteen hours ahead of Eastern Standard Time. Normal business hours are 8:30 a.m. - 5:00 p.m., Monday-Friday. Government of Singapore agencies and many private sector companies are closed for business on Saturday. Shops are normally open every day from 10:00 am – 9:00 p.m.

The American Embassy closes on American and local holidays. The dates on which holidays are observed in 2014 and 2015 are listed below:

2014

OFFICIAL DATE	U.S. HOLIDAY	SINGAPORE HOLIDAY	DATE OBSERVED
January 1	New Year's Day	New Year's Day	Wednesday, January 1
3rd Mon in January	Birthday of Martin Luther King, Jr.		Monday, January 20
January 31 (Friday) & February 1 (Saturday)		Chinese New Year	Thursday, January 30 Friday, January 31 Saturday, February 1
3rd Mon in Feb	President's Day		Monday, February 17

Official Date	U.S. Holiday	Singapore Holiday	Date Observed
April 18		Good Friday	Friday, April 18
May 1		Labor Day	Thursday, May 1
May 13		Vesak Day	Tuesday, May 13
Last Mon in May	Memorial Day		Monday, May 26
July 4	Independence Day		Friday, July 4
July 28		Hari Raya Puasa	Monday, July 28
August 9 (Saturday)		National Day	Friday, August 8
1st Mon in September	Labor Day		Monday, September 1
October 5 (Sunday)		Hari Raya Haji	Monday, October 6
2nd Mon in October	Columbus Day		Monday, October 13
October 22		Deepavali	Wednesday, October 22
November 11	Veteran's Day		Tuesday, November 11
4th Thu in November	Thanksgiving		Thursday, November 27
December 25	Christmas	Christmas	Thursday, December 25

<u>2015</u>

OFFICIAL DATE	U.S. HOLIDAY	SINGAPORE HOLIDAY	DATE OBSERVED
January 1	New Year's Day	New Year's Day	Thursday, January 1
3rd Mon in January	Birthday of Martin Luther King, Jr.		Monday, January 19
3rd Mon in	President's Day		Monday, February

Date	Holiday		Observed
February			16
February 19 & February 20		Chinese New Year	Thursday, February 19 Friday, February 20
April 3		Good Friday	Friday, April 3
May 1		Labor Day	Friday, May 1
Last Monday in May	Memorial Day		Monday, May 25
June 1		Vesak Day	Monday, June 1
July 4	Independence Day		Friday, July 3
July 17		Hari Raya Puasa	Friday, July 17
August 9		National Day	Sunday, August 9 Monday, August 10
1st Mon in September	Labor Day		Monday, September 7
September 24		Hari Raya Haji	Thursday, September 24
2nd Mon in October	Columbus Day		Monday, October 12
November 10		Deepavali	Tuesday, November 10
November 11	Veteran's Day		Wednesday, November 11
4th Thu in November	Thanksgiving		Thursday, November 26
December 25	Christmas	Christmas	Friday, December 25

Temporary Entry of Materials and Personal Belongings Return to top

Goods may be temporarily imported under the Temporary Import Scheme for the purpose of repairs, displays, exhibitions or other similar events without the payment of import duty and/or GST. A banker's guarantee is required under the Temporary Import Scheme. The temporary imports are covered by a Customs Inward Permit or a Carnet. Goods temporarily imported must be re-exported within the prescribed period using a Customs Outward permit. GST has to be paid if the goods are not subsequently re-exported. The procedures governing such importation can be found at http://www.customs.gov.sg/leftNav/trad/Temporary+Import+Scheme.htm

Web Resources Return to top

http://www.ida.gov.sg/Infocomm-Landscape/Infrastructure/Wireless/Wireless-at-SG/For-Consumer

http://travel.state.gov/

http://travel.state.gov/travel/tips/safety/safety_1747.html

http://www.customs.gov.sg/topNav/hom/

http://www.mfa.gov.sg/washington/

http://travel.state.gov/travel/cis_pa_tw/cis/cis_1017.html

http://www.cdc.gov/travel/seasia.htm

http://travel.state.gov/visa/

http://wwwn.cdc.gov/travel/default.aspx

http://www.who.int/en

http://www.who.int/ith

http://www.moh.gov.sg/

Return to table of contents

Return to table of contents

Chapter 9: Contacts, Market Research and Trade Events

- Contacts
- Market Research
- Trade Events

Contacts   Return to top

Singapore Government directory of senior officers, including their contact details can be found online at www.sgdi.gov.sg

Major Singapore Government agencies:

Accounting & Corporate Regulatory Authority – http://www.acra.gov.sg
Agency for Science, Technology and Research (ASTAR) – http://www.a-star.edu.sg
Agri-Food & Veterinary Authority of Singapore – http://www.ava.gov.sg
Building & Construction Authority – http://www.bca.gov.sg
Board of Architects – http://www.boa.gov.sg
Casino Regulatory Authority of Singapore – http://www.cra.gov.sg/
Central Provident Fund Board – http://www.cpf.gov.sg
Centre for Drug Administration (CDA) – http://www.hsa.gov.sg
Centre for Forensic Medicine (CFM) – http://www.hsa.gov.sg
Centre for Medical Device Regulation (CMDR) – http://www.hsa.gov.sg
Civil Aviation Authority of Singapore – http://www.caas.gov.sg
Civil Service College – http://www.cscollege.gov.sg/
Competition Commission of Singapore - http://www.ccs.gov.sg
Council for Estate Agencies - http://www.cea.gov.sg/
Council for Private Education - http://www.cpe.gov.sg/
Defense Science & Technology Agency - http://www.dsta.gov.sg/
Economic Development Board – http://sedb.com
Energy Market Authority - http://www.ema.gov.sg/
Health Promotion Board – http://www.hpb.gov.sg
Health Sciences Authority - http://www.hsa.gov.sg
Housing And Development Board – http://hdb.gov.sg
Immigration & Checkpoints Authority – http://www.ica.gov.sg
Infocomm Development Authority of Singapore – http://www.ida.gov.sg
Inland Revenue Authority of Singapore – http://www.iras.gov.sg
Institute for Infocomm Research – http://www.i2r.a-star.edu.sg
Institute of Microelectronics – http://www.ime.a-star.edu.sg
Institute of Technical Education – http://www.ite.edu.sg
Intellectual Property Office of Singapore – http://www.ipos.gov.sg
International Enterprise Singapore – http://www.iesingapore.gov.sg
JTC Corporation – http://www.jtc.gov.sg
Land Transport Authority (LTA) – http://www.lta.gov.sg
Media Development Authority – http://www.mda.gov.sg
Maritime and Port Authority of Singapore - http://www.mpa.gov.sg/

Ministry of Communications and Information – http://www.mci.gov.sg/
Ministry of Culture, Community & Youth – http://www.mccy.gov.sg/
Ministry of Defence – http://www.mindef.gov.sg
Ministry of Education – http://www.moe.edu.sg
Ministry of Finance – http://www.mof.gov.sg
Ministry of Foreign Affairs – http://www.mfa.gov.sg
Ministry of Health – http://www.moh.gov.sg
Ministry of Home Affairs – http://www.mha.gov.sg
Ministry of Law – http://www.minlaw.gov.sg
Ministry of Manpower – http://www.mom.gov.sg
Ministry of National Development – http://www.mnd.gov.sg
Ministry of the Environment and Water Resources – http://www.mewr.gov.sg
Ministry of Social & Family Development - http://www.msf.gov.sg/
Ministry of Trade and Industry – http://www.mti.gov.sg
Ministry of Transport – http://www.mot.gov.sg
Monetary Authority of Singapore – http://www.mas.gov.sg
National Environment Agency - http://www.nea.gov.sg
National Library Board - http://www.nlb.gov.sg/
National Parks Board - http://www.nparks.gov.sg
National Arts Council – http://www.nac.gov.sg
Personal Data Protection Commission – http://www.pdpc.gov.sg
PSA Corporation Limited – http://www.psa.com.sg
PUB, The National Water Agency – http://www.pub.gov.sg
Sentosa Development Corporation - http://www.sentosa.com.sg
Singapore Customs – http://www.customs.gov.sg
Singapore Land Authority – http://www.sla.gov.sg
Singapore Sports Council – http://www.ssc.gov.sg
Singapore Tourism Board – http://www.stb.com.sg
Singapore Workforce Development Agency - http://www.wda.gov.sg/
Spring Singapore – http://www.spring.gov.sg
Urban Redevelopment Authority – http://www.ura.gov.sg

Singapore government website – http://www.gov.sg

Trade Associations/Chambers of Commerce in Singapore

American Chamber of Commerce in Singapore – http://www.amcham.org.sg
Association of Process Industry – http://www.aspri.com.sg
Association of Small and Medium Enterprises – http://www.asme.org.sg
Association of the Telecommunications Industry of Singapore – http://www.atis.org.sg
General Insurance Association of Singapore – http://www.gia.org.sg
The Institution of Engineers, Singapore – http://www.ies.org.sg
Instrumentation & Control Society Singapore – http://www.singics.org.sg
Life Insurance Association Singapore – http://www.lia.org.sg
Motor Traders Association of Singapore – http://www.mta.org.sg
Packaging Council of Singapore – http://www.packaging.org.sg
Real Estate Developers' Association of Singapore – http://www.redas.com
Recording Industry Association (Singapore) – http://www.rias.org.sg
Singapore Association of Pharmaceutical Industries (SAPI) – http://www.sapi.org.sg
Singapore Business Federation – http://www.sbf.org.sg

Singapore Chinese Chamber of Commerce and Industry – http://www.sccci.org.sg
Singapore Computer Society – http://www.scs.org.sg
Singapore Cycle & Motor Traders' Association – http://www.autoparts.com.sg
Singapore Dental Association – http://www.sda.org.sg
Singapore Exchange Ltd. – http://www.sgx.com
Singapore Furniture Industries Council – http://www.singaporefurniture.com
Singapore Indian Chamber of Commerce and Industry – http://www.sicci.com
Singapore Industrial Automation Association – http://www.siaa.org
Singapore Infocomm Technology Federation – http://www.sitf.org.sg
Singapore Institute of Architects – http://www.sia.org.sg
Singapore Institute of Planners- http://www.sip.org.sg
Singapore Institute of Surveyors & Valuers – http://www.sisv.org.sg
Singapore International Chamber of Commerce – http://www.sicc.com.sg
Singapore Jewellers Association – http://www.sja.org.sg
Singapore Malay Chamber of Commerce – http://www.smcci.org.sg
Singapore Manufacturing Federation – http://www.smafederation.org.sg
Singapore Medical Association – http://www.sma.org.sg
Singapore Plastic Industry Association – http://www.spia.org.sg
Singapore Precision Engineering & Tooling Association – http://www.speta.org
Singapore Retailers Association – http://www.retail.org.sg/
Singapore Shipping Association – http://www.ssa.org.sg
Singapore Society of Radiographers – http://ssr.org.sg/
Textile and Fashion Federation (Singapore) – http://www.taff.org.sg
The Association of Banks in Singapore – http://www.abs.org.sg
The Singapore Contractors Association Ltd. – http://www.scal.com.sg
US - Asean Business Council, Inc. – http://www.usasean.org/countries/singapore

U.S. Commercial Service Singapore – www.export.gov/singapore

Singapore website - http://www.sg

Market Research   Return to top

To view market research reports produced by the U.S. Commercial Service please go to the following website: http://www.export.gov/mrktresearch/index.asp and click on Country and Industry Market Reports.

Please note that these reports are only available to U.S. citizens and U.S. companies. Registration to the site is required, and is free.

`Trade Events   Return to top

Please click on the link below for information on upcoming trade events.

http://www.export.gov/tradeevents/index.asp

http://export.gov/singapore/tradeevents/index.asp

Chapter 10: Guide to Our Services

The President's National Export Initiative marshals Federal agencies to **prepare U.S. companies to export successfully**, **connect them with trade opportunities** and **support them once they do have exporting opportunities**.

The U.S. Commercial Service offers customized solutions to help U.S. exporters, particularly small and medium sized businesses, successfully expand exports to new markets. Our global network of trade specialists will work one-on-one with you through every step of the exporting process, helping you to:

- Target the best markets with our world-class research
- Promote your products and services to qualified buyers
- Meet the best distributors and agents for your products and services
- Overcome potential challenges or trade barriers
- Gain access to the full range of U.S. government trade promotion agencies and their services, including export training and potential trade financing sources

To learn more about the Federal Government's trade promotion resources for new and experienced exporters, please click on the following link: www.export.gov

For more information on the services the U.S. Commercial Service offers to U.S. exporters, please click on the following link:
http://export.gov/singapore/servicesforu.s.companies/index.asp

U.S. exporters seeking general export information/assistance or country-specific commercial information can also contact the **U.S. Department of Commerce's Trade Information Center** at **(800) USA-TRAD(E).**

To the best of our knowledge, the information contained in this report is accurate as of the date published. However, **The Department of Commerce** does not take responsibility for actions readers may take based on the information contained herein. Readers should always conduct their own due diligence before entering into business ventures or other commercial arrangements. **The Department of Commerce** can assist companies in these endeavors.